Bond Assessment Papers

Fourth papers in Mathematics

J M Bond and Andrew Baines

Key words

Some special maths words are used in this book. You will find them **in bold** the first time they appear in the papers. These words are explained here.

acute angle	an angle that is less than a right angle
co-ordinates	the two numbers, the first horizontal the second vertical, that plot a point on a grid. e.g. (3, 2)
factor	the factors of a number are numbers that divide into it. e.g. 1, 2, 4 and 8 are all factors of 8.
kite	a four-sided shape that looks like a stretched diamond
lowest term	the simplest you can make a fraction. e.g. $\frac{4}{10}$ reduced to the lowest term is $\frac{2}{5}$.
mean	one kind of average. You find the mean by adding all the scores together and dividing by the number of scores. e.g. The mean of 1, 3 and 8 is 4.
median	one kind of average, the middle number of a set of numbers after being ordered from lowest to highest. e.g. The median of 1, 3 and 8 is 3. e.g. The median of 7, 4, 6 and 9 is 6.5 (half way between 6 and 7)
mixed number	a number that contains a whole number and a fraction. e.g $5\frac{1}{2}$ is a mixed number.
mode	one kind of average. The most common number in a set of numbers. e.g. The mode of 2, 3, 2, 7, 2 is 2.
obtuse angle	an angle that is more than 90° and not more than 180 degrees
polygon	a closed shape with many sides
prime factor	the factors of a number that are also prime numbers. e.g The prime factors of 12 are 2 and 3.
prime numbers	any number that can only be divided by itself or 1. 2, 3 and 7 are prime numbers. (Note that 1 is not a prime number.)
quotient	the answer if you divide one number by another. e.g. The quotient of 12 ÷ 4 is 3.
range	the difference between the largest and smallest of a set of numbers. e.g. The range of 1, 2, 5, 3, 6, 8 is 7.
reflex angle	an angle that is bigger than 180°
rhombus	a four sided shape, like a squashed square, that has all its sides of equal length and its opposite sides parallel
trapezium	a four-sided shape that has just one pair of parallel sides
vertex, vertices	the point where two or more edges or sides in a shape meet

Paper 1

1-5 Here is a pie chart which shows how Joanna spent yesterday evening between 6 p.m. and 8 p.m.

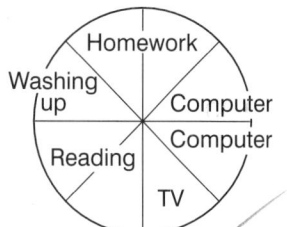

Joanna was watching TV for __15 mins__ doing homework for __30 mins__ reading for __30 mins__, washing up for __15 mins__ and was on the computer for __30 mins__ [5/5]

What is the average (**mean**) of the following numbers?

6	7 4 6 8 5	6
7	3 2 7	4
8	4 4 6 2	4

[3/3]

9 Make 999 ten times as large. __9990__ [1/1]

In each of the following lines underline the smallest number and put a ring round the largest number.

10-11 $\frac{5}{8}$ $\frac{3}{4}$ ⓐ$\frac{7}{8}$ $\frac{6}{8}$

12-13 3.07   3.7   ㉗   3.007   0.307

14-15 ⓐ$\frac{15}{3}$ $\frac{12}{6}$ $\frac{27}{9}$ $\frac{8}{2}$ $\frac{10}{10}$

16-17 0.125 $\frac{1}{2}$ 0.25   ⓐ$\frac{7}{8}$ 0.75

18-19 $\frac{3}{4}$ of 12 $\frac{5}{7}$ of 14 $\frac{2}{3}$ of 9 $\frac{2}{5}$ of 10   ⓐ$\frac{1}{2}$ of 16   [9/10]

20 Write in figures: one hundred and two thousand and twenty-one. __102 021__ [1]

21-24
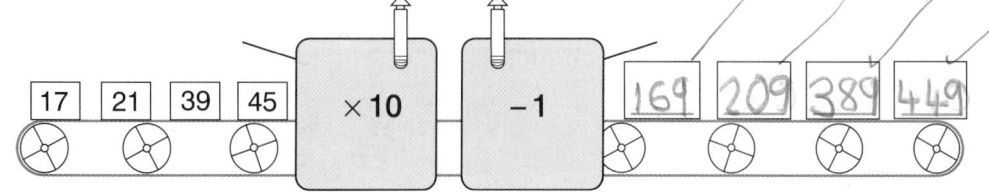
[4/4]

What is the size of the smaller angle:

25 between 1 and 3? __45°__ ✗
26 between 2 and 7? __170°__ ✗
27 between 7 and 11? __140°__ ✗
28 between 8 and 9? __40°__ ✗
29 between 4 and 10? __200°__ ✗

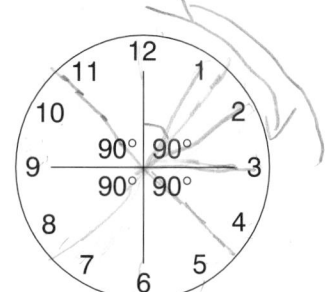

[0/5]

3

30 (7 × 8) + __5__ = 61
31 (9 × 12) − __2__ = 106
32 8 × (7 − __16__) = 32
33 6 × (11 − __30__) = 36

34–37 Plot the points (3,5), (−1,5), (3,−2) on the grid.

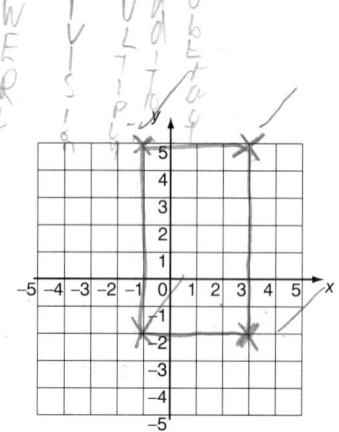

These points are the **vertices** of a rectangle. Mark the fourth vertex and draw the rectangle.

38 The **co-ordinates** of the fourth vertex are (__−2__ , __−1__).

Write the times which are a quarter of an hour before the following.

39 22:00   21:45
40 11:05   10:40
41 13:10   12:35

36 articles are shared among A, B and C in the ratio of 1:3:5.

42 How many articles does A have?
43 How many articles does B have?
44 How many articles does C have?

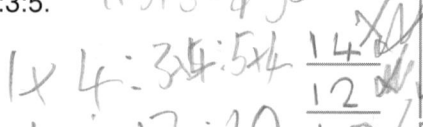

Put a sign in each space to make the sum correct.

45 45 __+__ 7 = 52   46 33 __÷__ 3 = 11
47 678 __×__ 56 = 37968   48 90 __÷__ 5 = 18

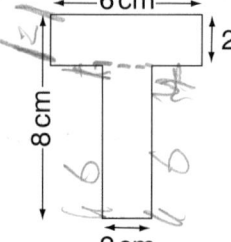

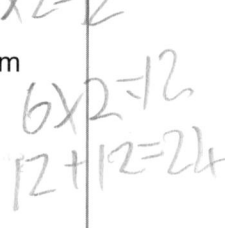

49 What is the area of this shape?   __80__ cm²
50 What is the perimeter of this shape? __18__ cm

4

Paper 2

Divide each of these numbers by 10.

1. 78.65   7.865
2. 6.54   0.654
3. 467.5   46.75
4. 0.123   0.0123

5–8 Work out these, and then write them out in order, from highest to lowest **quotient**.

$7)\overline{315}$ = 45 $8)\overline{392}$ = 49 $7)\overline{329}$ = 47 $9)\overline{387}$ = 43

$8)\overline{392}$ $7)\overline{329}$ $7)\overline{315}$ $9)\overline{387}$

9–10 In a school 6 out of every 11 children are girls.

If there are 407 children in the school there are: 185 boys and 222 girls.

11–12 Use the conversion graph to rewrite the road sign in kilometres.

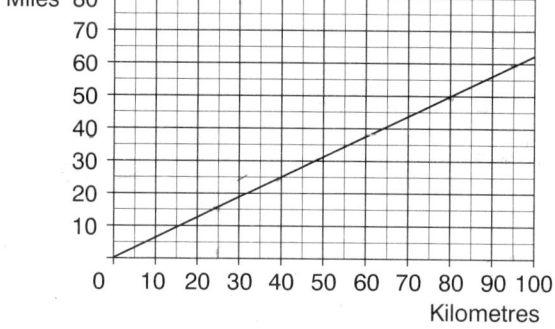

| Darlington | 25 miles |
| Newcastle | 50 miles |

| Darlington | 40 km |
| Newcastle | 80 km |

13 Approximately how many miles in 95 km?   60 miles
14 Which is the greater: 50 miles or 75 km?   50 miles

15–18 Put a sign in each space to make the sum correct.

74 ÷ 5 = 14.8   74 + 5 = 79

74 − 5 = 69   74 × 5 = 370

5

There are six balls, numbered 1 to 6, in a bag.

19 What is the probability that I will draw out an even-numbered ball?

20 What is the probability that I will draw out the 5?

21 What is the probability that I will draw out an odd-numbered ball?

22–24 Put a circle around each **prime number**.

3   4   5   6   7

25 What number is midway between 18 and 42?

26 What number is midway between 19 and 53?

27 Find the area of a square whose perimeter is 12 cm.

Using this world time chart answer the following.

| London | Austria | Cyprus | Hong Kong | Japan |
| 0 hr | +1 hr | +2 hr | +8 hr | +9 hr |

Sydney +10 hr

When it is midday in London it is:

28 9:00 pm in Japan.

29 2:00 pm in Cyprus.

30 1:00 pm in Austria.

31 8:00 pm in Hong Kong.

When it is midday in Japan it is:

32 3:00 am in London.

33 4:00 am in Hong Kong.

34 It is 12:00 in Cyprus. What time is it in Austria? 11:00

35 It is 4:36 p.m. in Hong Kong. What time is it in London? 6:36 am

36 $\frac{5}{8} + \frac{7}{16}$ =

37 $7 - 4\frac{2}{9}$ =

Some game cards are shared between Tom and Matthew in the ratio of 5:4.

38 If Matthew receives 16 Tom will get _____.

39 If they shared the same cards equally (not in 5:4) Matthew would receive _____.

The **median** is the middle number when a set of numbers are ordered from lowest to highest, e.g. the median of 8   4   7   is   7

40 The median of   1   3   8   is _____
41 The median of   20   34   11   is _____
42 The median of   4   3   3   is _____
43 The median of   5   9   3   7   6   is _____

44–46 Write these fractions as decimals.

$4\frac{1}{2}$ $7\frac{1}{10}$ $3\frac{9}{100}$

47–50 Complete these questions.

```
  887           378        12)2808         456
  998          ×  9                       × 35
+ 776
```

Paper 3

1 Which of the numbers in the oval is 2^2? _____
2 Which of the numbers in the oval is 5^2? _____
3 Which of the numbers in the oval is 3^2? _____
4 Which of the numbers in the oval is 6^2? _____

(oval containing: 20, 10, 25, 4, 36, 9, 18, 12, 8)

5–15 Complete this timetable for Merrywell School. There are five lessons each 35 minutes in length, with a break of 15 minutes after the third lesson.

	Begins	Ends
1st lesson	11:10	11:45
2nd lesson	11:45	12:20
3rd lesson	12:20	12:55
Break	12:55	1:10
4th lesson	1:10	1:45
5th lesson	1:45	2:20

16 What is the nearest number to 1000, but smaller than 1000, into which 38 will divide with no remainder? 760

What is the area of:

17 side A? 60 cm²
18 side B? 30 cm²
19 side C? 50 cm²

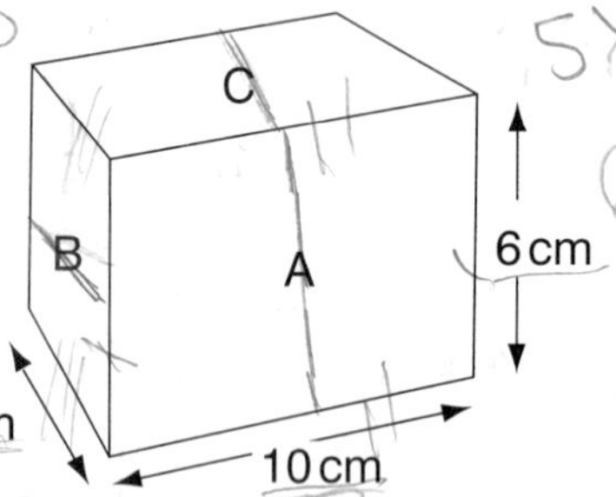

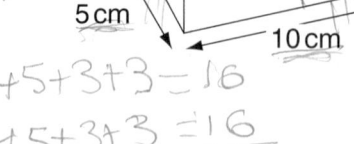

What is the perimeter of:

20 side A? 44 cm
21 side B? 32 cm
22 side C? 40 cm

23 $2 \times \triangle = 4 \times 5$ $\triangle = 10$
24 $5 \times \clubsuit = 27 - 2$ $\clubsuit = 5$
25 $\otimes \times 3 = 36 \div 3$ $\otimes = 4$
26 $\blacklozenge \times 4 = 10 + 10$ $\blacklozenge = 5$

Chris is 11 years old and Emma is 9.

They are given £40 to be shared between them in the ratio of their ages.

27 Chris will get
28 Emma will get

29 If 11 articles cost £7.37 what would be the cost of 8 articles? £5.36

Find the area of these triangles. The area of a triangle = $\frac{1}{2}$ (base × height)

Scale: 1 square = 1 cm²

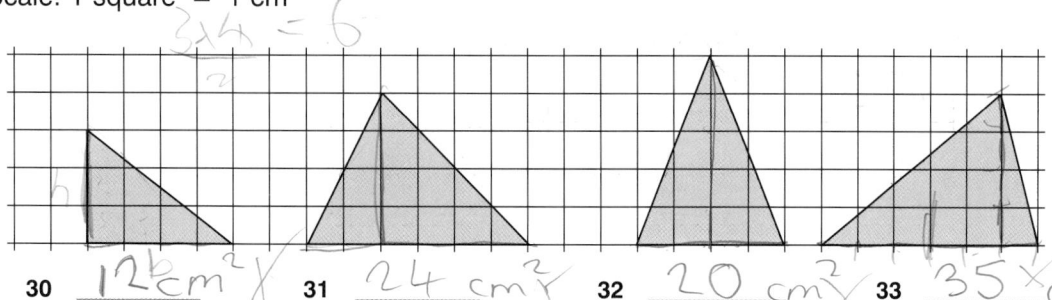

30 __12 cm²__   31 __24 cm²__   32 __20 cm²__   33 __35 cm²__

At our car park the charges are as follows:

Up to 1 hour	£1.00
Over 1 hour and up to 2 hours	£1.75
Over 2 hours and up to 4 hours	£3.50
Over 4 hours and up to 6 hours	£5.25
Over 6 hours and up to 8 hours	£7.00

34 Miss Short parks her car at 12:30 p.m. and collects it at 4 p.m. How much will she have to pay?   __£3.50__

35 Mrs Rowlands parks her car at 9:15 a.m. and collects it at 11:30 a.m. How much will she have to pay?   __£3.50__

36 Mr Reads parks his car at 2:20 p.m. and collects it at 6:30 p.m. How much will he have to pay?   __£5.25__

37 Mr Davies parks his car at 8:45 a.m. and collects it at 4:30 p.m. How much will he have to pay?   __£7.00__

38–43 VAT (Value Added Tax) is charged at $17\frac{1}{2}$% on some goods.

This means that a £100.00 article would have a tax of £17.50 added to its cost.
Complete the table below.

Price before VAT	VAT	Total cost
£200.00	£35	£235.00
£400.00	£70	£470.00
£300.00	£50.50	£350.50

44
```
  m  cm
  4  72
+ 3  39
-------
  8  21 cm
```

45
```
  m  cm
  5  6¹2
- 3   8
-------
  2  6 cm
```

46
```
  m  cm
  4  60
×    5
-------
 23 00 cm
```

47–50 Write these numbers to the nearest 100.

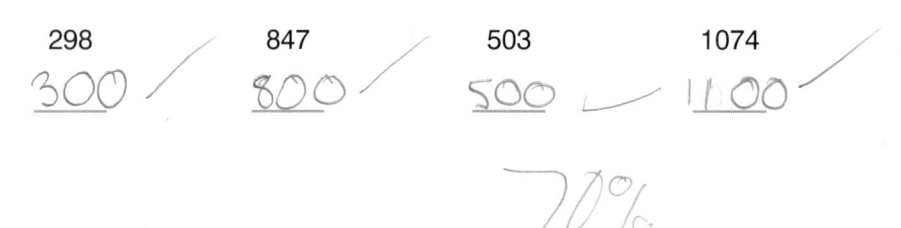

298   847   503   1074
_300_   _800_   _500_   _1100_

Paper 4

1–5 Fill in the gaps.

	Length	Width	Perimeter
Rectangle 1	18 cm	_13_ cm	40 cm
Rectangle 2	_8_ cm	3 cm	30 cm
Rectangle 3	9 cm	4 cm	_22_ cm
Square	6 cm	_6_ cm	_24_ cm

6 How many times can 28 be subtracted from 1316?   _47_

7–12 Ring the correct answer in each line.

0.1 × 0.1 =	0.2	0.02	(0.01)	0.1	1.1
10% of 40 =	8	5	80	20	(4)
10 – 9.99 =	0.9	(0.01)	1.00	1.1	1.9
0.207 ÷ 0.3 =	0.9	0.09	(0.69)	0.66	0.23
1.1 × 1.1 =	(1.21)	1.11	11.1	2.2	1.01
567 ÷ 100 =	56 700	0.567	56.7	(5.67)	5670

13 The product of two numbers is 1260. One of the numbers is 35.
What is the other number?   _36_

14–20 Write the missing digits or answer.

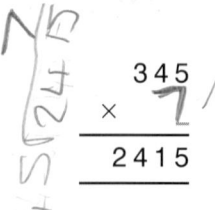

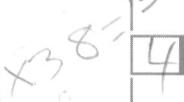

```
  5365           1 7_           345          38
  27_1         -  2_5         ×    7       9)342
+ 345_          -----          -----
 -----           786           2415
 10603
```

Find the value of y in the following equations.

21 $3y = 10 - 1$
    $y = 3$

22 $4y - y = 12$
    $y = $ ___

23 $2y + y = 6$
    $y = 4$

24 $3y + y = 11 + 1$
    $y = $ ___

A coin is tossed at the start of a game. Underline the correct answer to each question.

25 What is the probability of getting a head?
    $\frac{2}{3}$ $\frac{4}{5}$ $\underline{\frac{1}{2}}$ $\frac{3}{4}$

26 What is the probability of getting a tail?
    $\frac{2}{3}$ $\frac{4}{5}$ $\underline{\frac{1}{2}}$ $\frac{3}{4}$

A fair dice numbered 1 to six is rolled at the start of a game. Underline the correct answer to each question.

27 What is the probability of getting a 6?
    $\frac{2}{3}$ $\underline{\frac{1}{6}}$ $\frac{1}{2}$ $\frac{3}{4}$

28 What is the probability of getting a 5?
    $\frac{1}{3}$ $\frac{1}{4}$ $\frac{1}{5}$ $\frac{1}{6}$

29 What is the probability of getting a 2 or a 3?
    $\frac{1}{6}$ $\underline{\frac{1}{3}}$ $\frac{1}{2}$ $\frac{2}{3}$

A bag contains 4 grey balls and 3 white balls. Underline the correct answer to each question.

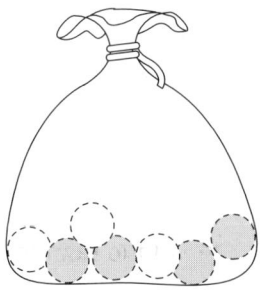

30 What is the probability of picking a white ball?
    $\frac{3}{4}$ $\frac{3}{5}$ $\frac{3}{6}$ $\underline{\frac{3}{7}}$ $\frac{3}{8}$

31 What is the probability of picking a grey ball?
    0 $\frac{1}{2}$ $\underline{\frac{4}{7}}$ $\frac{3}{7}$ $\frac{3}{4}$

32 What is the probability of picking a black ball?
    $\underline{0}$ $\frac{1}{2}$ $\frac{4}{7}$ $\frac{3}{7}$ $\frac{3}{4}$

11

Multiply each of these numbers by 10.

33 3.77   37.7
34 46.5   465
35 0.126 1.26
36 0.027 0.27
37 49   490
38 567   5670
39 0.0023 0.023

The median of 2 3 4 5 is 3.5 (halfway between 3 and 4)
The median of 7 4 6 9 is 6.5 (halfway between 6 and 7)

Find the median of the following.

40 4   6   8   10
41 8   2   6   8
42 54 21 7   19
43 1   2   3   4   5   6
44 32 21 60 3   5   17
45 45 47

Change these 24-hour times into 12-hour times using a.m. or p.m.

46 05:05 am
47 12:45 pm
48 20:02 pm
49 15:15 pm
50 11:14 am

Paper 5

1–7 Complete the following chart.

	Length	Width	Area
Rectangle 1	8 m	6 m	48 m²
Rectangle 2	8m	4 m	32 m²
Rectangle 3	4 m	6m	10 m²
Rectangle 4	6m	3.5 m	10.5 m²
Rectangle 5	1.5 m	1.5 m	2.25 m²
Rectangle 6	5 m	1.5m	6 m²
Rectangle 7	1.3 m	2 m	2.6 m²

Find the area of these triangles. The area of a triangle = $\frac{1}{2}$ (base × height)

Scale: 1 square = 1 cm²

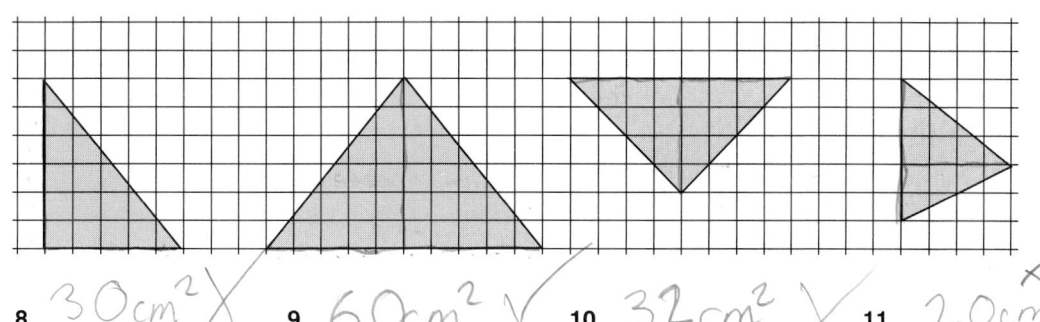

8 30 cm²   9 60 cm²   10 32 cm²   11 20 cm²

12 My watch loses a quarter of a minute every hour. If I put it right at midday, what time will my watch show at 8 p.m. that evening? 19.58

A class carried out a survey to find the most popular subject.

Favourite subject	Votes
English	5
Mathematics	12
PE	7
Music	6

13 Which is the most popular subject? Mathematics
14 Which is the least popular subject? English
15 How many votes are there in total? 30
16 What is the mean number of votes? 9

17–22 Complete the table.

∇	2	4	6	8	10	12
2 × ∇ =	4	8	12	16	20	24

Reduce these prices by 10%.

23 £50   £45
24 £110 £99
25 £250 £225
26 £40   £36
27 £30   £27
28 £280 £252

29–30 One day 20% of the children were away from school on a visit to a museum.
If there were 360 children altogether, __288__ children were in school and __72__ were on the museum trip.

31 A number multiplied by itself is 16. What is the number? __4__

£1	=	1.46 US Dollars
£1	=	119 Kenyan Shillings
£1	=	1.42 Euros
£1	=	2.13 Australian Dollars

32 How many US Dollars do you get for £10? __14.6__
33 How many Kenyan Shillings do you get for £100? __11900__
34 How many Euros do you get for £1000? __1420__
35 How many Australian Dollars do you get for £100 000? __213000__
36 How many US Dollars do you get for £20? __29.2__
37 How many Kenyan Shillings do you get for £400? __47600__

38 What number when divided by 12, has an answer 11 remainder 5? __137__

12 × 11 = 132 + 5 = 137

A concert starts at 7:30 p.m. The first half of the programme lasts 1 hour 35 minutes, then there is an interval of 8 minutes.

39 When does the second half of the concert begin? __9:13__

A rectangular field is 3 times as long as it is wide. If the perimeter is 0.8 km:

40 what is the length? __3 km__
41 what is the width? __1 km__
42 what is the area? __6 km²__

43 I have enough tinned dog food to last my 2 dogs 18 days. If I got another dog how long would this food last? __9 days__

44 Add the greatest to the smallest.
565   656   556   655   566   665   __1221__

45 What number is halfway between 37 and 111? __64__

46–47 Put a circle around the prime numbers.
12   ⑬   14   15   16   ⑰   18

48–50 What are the **prime factors** of 60? __2__ and __3__ and __5__

Paper 6

1–3

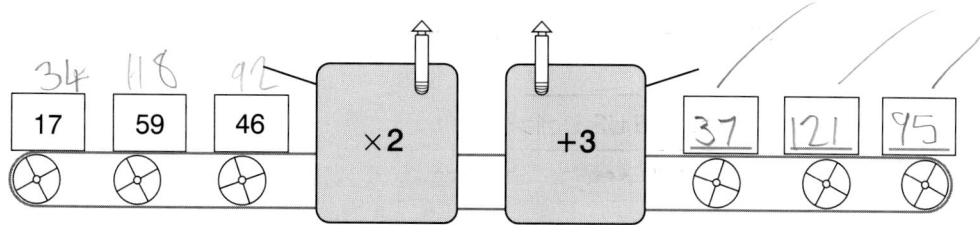

4–8 Here are five 'regular **polygons**' (polygons with sides of equal length and whose angles are all equal).

Give the size of each angle at the centre of the polygon.

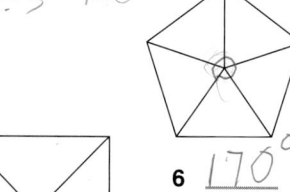

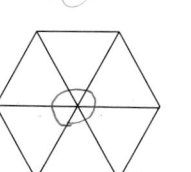

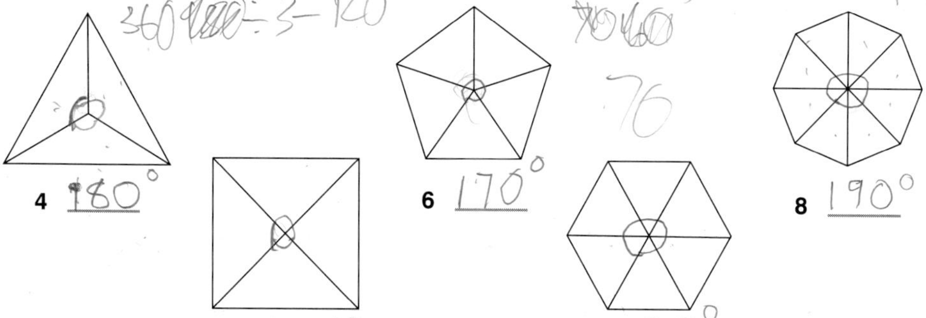

4 180°   5 175°   6 170°   7 185°   8 190°

Convert the following lengths to metres.

9 245 cm = 2.45 m   10 1342 cm = 13.42 m

11 12 345 cm = 123.45 m

Convert the following lengths to kilometres.

12 1357 m = 1.357 km   13 12 986 m = 12.986 km

14 456 m = 0.456 km

15–16 There are 30 children in Class 4. 60% of them are girls.

There are 8 girls and 12 boys.

17 Which number, when multiplied by 30, will give the same answer as 51 × 10?   510 ÷ 30 = 17

18 Write the number which is 7 less than 2000.   1993

19–34 Insert a sign in each space so that the answer given for each line and column is correct.

3	×	3	−	2	=	7
×		+		×		−
6	+	4	−	5	=	5
÷		−		−		×
2	×	5	−	4	=	6
=		=		=		=
9	×	2	−	6	=	12

35 If 9 articles cost £6.30, what will be the cost of 11 articles?   £7.70

Here is a list of some of the longest rivers in the world.
Write the length of each river to the nearest 1000 km.

36 Amazon   6516 km   7000 km
37 Chang Jiang   6380 km   6000 km
38 Nile   6695 km   7000 km
39 Paraná   4500 km   5000 km
40 Mississippi–Missouri 6019 km   6000 km
41 Zaire   4667 km   5000 km

Fill in the spaces with one of these signs   <   >   =

42 8 × 9   =   6 × 12
43 8 + 9 + 7   <   30 − 3
44 0.5 m   >   45 cm
45 23   > 3^2
46 12^2 <   144
47 50 min   > $\frac{3}{4}$ hour

Consider a dice numbered 1 to 6.
What is the probability of rolling:

48 a 4 or a 5?   1/6
49 a 7?   0
50 a whole number greater than 0 and less than 7?   6/6

16

Paper 7

Underline the correct answer in each line.

1. $0.2 \times 0.2 =$ 0.4   4   40   <u>0.04</u>   0.004
2. $\frac{1}{2} + \frac{1}{4} =$ $\frac{2}{6}$ <u>$\frac{3}{4}$</u> $\frac{2}{4}$ $\frac{2}{8}$ $\frac{1}{8}$
3. 50% of 30 =   35   20   25   130   <u>15</u>
4. $10 \div \frac{1}{2} =$ <u>20</u>   5 $10\frac{1}{2}$ $\frac{1}{20}$ $\frac{1}{5}$
5. $5 \div 0.5 =$ 0.1   0.01   100   <u>10</u>   0.001
6. $412 \div 4 =$ 13   <u>103</u>   104   12   14
7. $\frac{1}{8} + \frac{1}{2} =$ $\frac{1}{16}$ $\frac{1}{10}$ <u>$\frac{5}{8}$</u> $\frac{1}{2}$ $\frac{3}{8}$

Three buses leave the bus station at 7 a.m.

Service A runs every 5 minutes.

Service B runs every 15 minutes.

Service C runs every 12 minutes.

8. At what time will all three services again start from the bus station at the same time?   8 a.m

Here is a list of some of the highest mountains in the world.

Write the height of each mountain to the nearest 1000 feet.

9. Aconcagua   22 834 feet   23,000 feet
10. Everest   29 028 feet   29,000 feet
11. K2   28 250 feet   28,000 feet
12. Kilimanjaro   19 340 feet   19,000 feet
13. McKinley   20 320 feet   20,000 feet
14. Mont Blanc   15 744 feet   16,000 feet

15. What number, when multiplied by 10, has the same answer as 15×12?   18

16–18 Andrew has half as many computer games as Stuart, who has half as many as Meena. Together they have 140 computer games.
Meena has 80 computer games, Stuart has 40 and Andrew has 20.

17

Here is a record of attendance of 40 children for one week of the term.

Attendance	Mon	Tues	Wed	Thurs	Fri
Morning	36	33	37	34	35
Afternoon	39	36	38	36	36

19. What was the mean (average) morning attendance?
20. What was the median afternoon attendance?
21. What was the mode afternoon attendance?

Multiply each of the numbers below by 1000.

22. 37.8
23. 2.45
24. 0.047
25. 25.0
26. 0.82
27. $7\frac{7}{8} + 5\frac{13}{16} =$
28. $7\frac{1}{5} - 3\frac{11}{15} =$

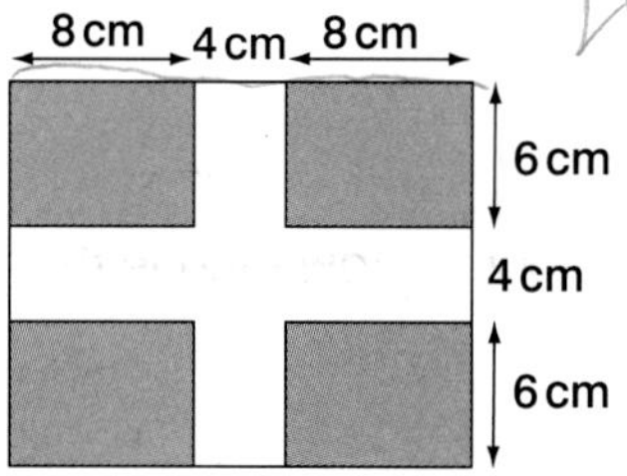

29. What is the total area of the flag?
30. What is the area of the cross?
31. What is the area of the grey area?
32. What is the perimeter of the flag?
33. What is the perimeter of the cross?

Label the following angles. Choose from: **acute, obtuse, reflex** or **right angle**.

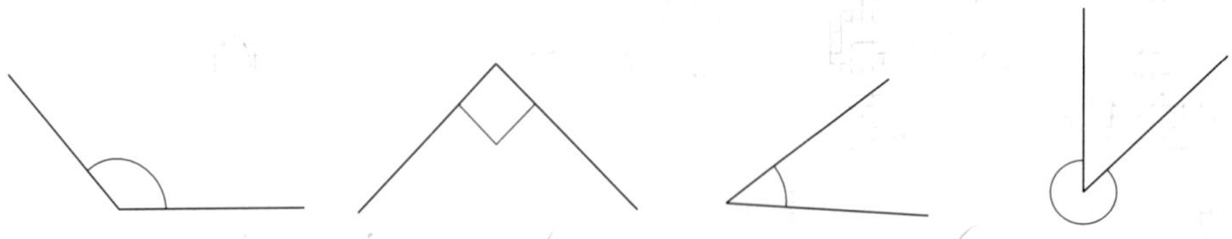

34. obtuse   35. right angle   36. acute   37. reflex

Here are a series of triangles. The first triangle has one row and one dot. The second triangle has 2 rows and 4 (or 2^2) dots. The third triangle has 3 rows and 9 (or 3^2) dots.

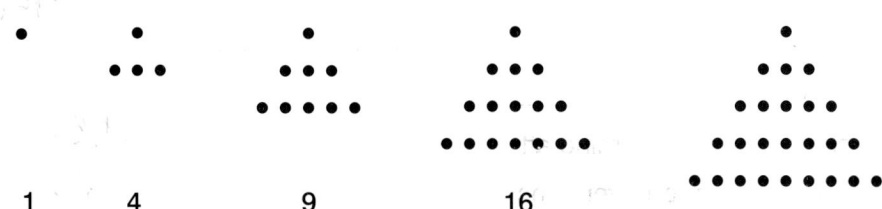

1   4   9   16

38 How many dots are there in 5 rows?   25
39 If there were 7 rows how many dots would there be?   49
40 In 11 rows there would be __121__ dots.
41 In 20 rows there would be __400__ dots.

42 Which is more: 10 lb of carrots or 10 kg of carrots?   10 kg
43 Which is shorter: 14 km or 10 miles?   14 km
44 Which is greater: 2 litres or 2 pints?   2 pints

45 25 telegraph posts are spaced equally along the side of a road.
    If there is 85 m between each pair of posts, how long is that stretch of road?   21.25 m

46 A man's salary was £16 000. He is given a 5% increase.
    What is his new salary?   £16 005

47 A cricketer's average score for 6 innings is 12 runs.
    What must he score in his next innings to make his average 13?   8

48 Add together 4.5 m, 16.7 m and 127.09 m   148.29

49–50 Complete the drawings below using the line of symmetry marked by the dashes.

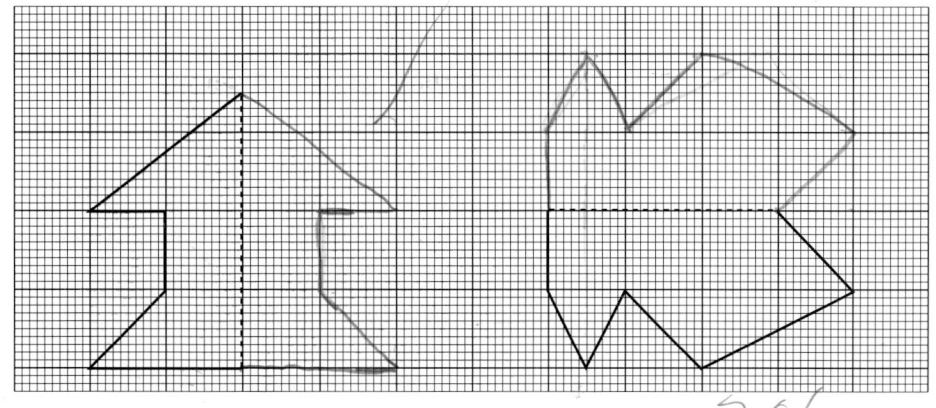

19

Paper 8

1. What is the difference between 0.225 tonnes and 128 kg?
2. If a = 2 and b = 3 find the value of 4a – 2b =
3. A book has 38 lines to each page.
   On which page will the 1000th line appear?

Change these 12-hour times into 24-hour times.

4. 10.10 a.m.
5. 11.20 p.m.
6. 1.01 a.m.
7. 7.45 p.m.

8–22

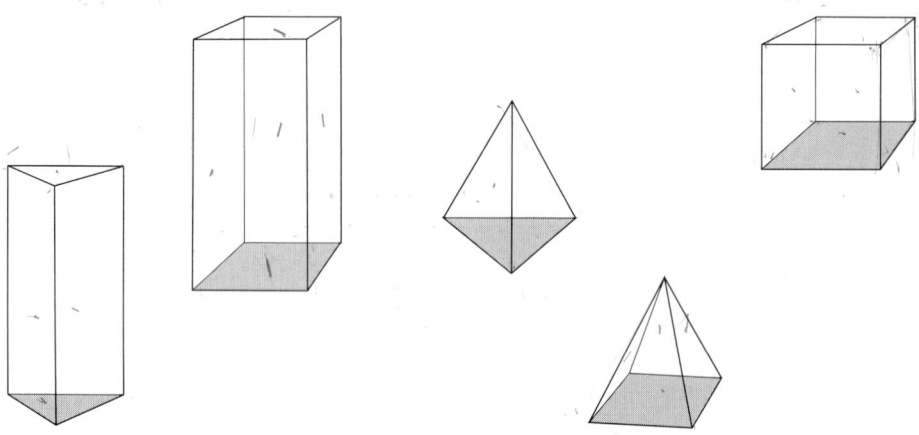

Name of solid	Number of faces	Number of vertices	Number of edges
Triangular prism	5	6	9
Square prism	6	8	12
Triangular pyramid	4	4	6
Square pyramid	5	5	8
Cube	6	8	12

23. Mrs Forgetmenot is 9 minutes late for the 9.42 a.m. train.
    How long will she have to wait for the train at 10.27 a.m.?

24–28 Local clubs took part in a 'clean the beach' campaign. Find out the percentage of members of each club which took part in this activity.

Club	Number of members	Number who took part	Percentage
A	100	79	79%
B	50	36	72%
C	150	120	80%
D	70	49	70%
E	80	60	75%

29 If $x = 5$ and $y = 2$ $\quad \dfrac{4x}{5y} = $ 2

30–40 Complete the timetable for Workmore School.

There are five lessons, each 30 minutes long, with a break of 15 minutes after the third lesson.

	Begins	Ends
1st lesson	9:40	10:10
2nd lesson	10:10	10:40
3rd lesson	10:40	11:10
Break	11:10	11:25
4th lesson	11:25	11:55
5th lesson	11:55	12:25

41 3 whole numbers multiplied together total 2475. Two of the numbers are 25 and 11. What is the third number?   9

42–43 5 is a prime factor of 2475.
What are the other two prime factors?   3 and 11

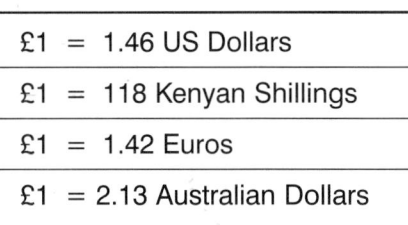

44 How many US Dollars do you get for £3?   4.38

45 How many Kenyan Shillings do you get for £1.50?

46 How many Euros do you get for £13?

47 How many Australian Dollars do you get for £50?

There are 351 children in a school. There are 7 boys to every 6 girls.

48 How many boys are there?

49 How many girls are there?

A number multiplied by itself and then doubled is 242.

50 What is the number?

Paper 9

Use these words to help you name the following shapes:
rhombus, kite, parallelogram, trapezium, rectangle.

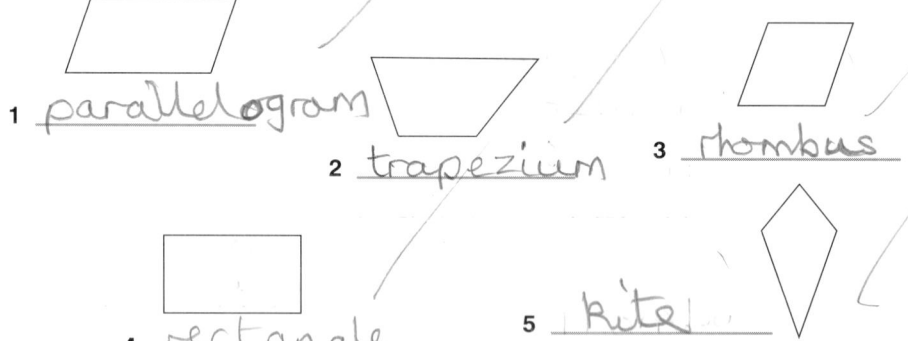

1 parallelogram
2 trapezium
3 rhombus
4 rectangle
5 kite

On one day in February the temperatures in different places were:

| Chicago | −3°C | Montreal | −10°C | Singapore | 31°C |
| Cape Town | 27°C | Miami | 26°C | Toronto | −5°C |

6 Which was the hottest of these places?
7 Which was the coldest?
8 How much colder was it in Chicago than Cape Town?
9 The difference between Toronto and Miami was
10 The difference between Singapore and Montreal was

11 Form the largest number possible with the digits 3, 9, 7 and 2 and then take away the smallest possible number. What is your answer?   7353

12 How many comics, costing 70p each, can be bought for £15.00?   21

13 In a certain question Amanda multiplied by 7 instead of dividing by 7. Her answer was 6027. What should it have been?

y × 7 = 6027 ✗   y ÷ 7 = 123 ✓

14–23 Write the next two numbers in each line.

3½	4¼	5	5¾	6½	7¼
100	90	81	73	64	58 ✗
47	52	58	65	73	82
2	5	11	20	32	48 ✗
2	4	8	16	32	64

24–25 The perimeter of a rectangular piece of paper is 48 cm. The length is 3 times the width. The length is 18 cm and the width is 6 cm

26–30

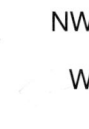

You start facing	turn through	clockwise/ anticlockwise	you are now facing
W	135°	anticlockwise	SE
SE	45°	clockwise	S
NE	90°	anticlockwise	NW
SW	45°	anticlockwise	S
S	180°	clockwise	N

31–34 3 pencils and 4 ballpoint pens cost £1.70p
3 pencils and 2 ballpoint pens cost £1.30p
Use this information to find the cost of:

2 ballpoint pens   40p   1 ballpoint pen   20p
3 pencils   90p   1 pencil   30p

23

90p + 80p = 1.70   90p + 40p = 1.30

35–38 Divide each of the following numbers by 1000.

385   0.385   0.12   0.00012

7.8   0.0078   49   0.049

The population of Grangetown is 11 552. The men and children together number 8763, and the men and women number 5874.   2889 M

39 How many women are there?   2985 W   2789

40 There are 5678 children.   5678 C

41 How many men are there?   3085

'The **factors** of 8 are 1, 2, 4 and 8.'

Find the following:

42 The factors of 12 are 1, 2, __3__, __4__, __6__ and __12__.

43 The factors of 20 are 1, __2__, __4__, __5__, __10__ and __20__.

44 The factors of 15 are __1__, __3__, __5__ and __15__.

45 The numbers that are factors of both 12 and 20 are 1, __2__ and __4__.

46 The numbers that are factors of both 12 and 15 are 1 and __3__.

47 The numbers that are factors of both 20 and 15 are 1 and __5__.

48–50 Now fill in the lengths of the sides of the box using these answers.

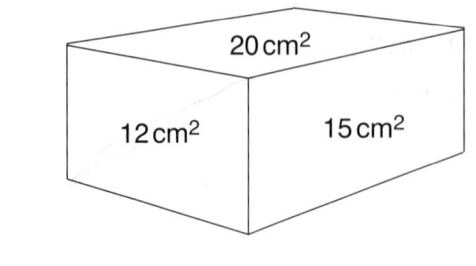

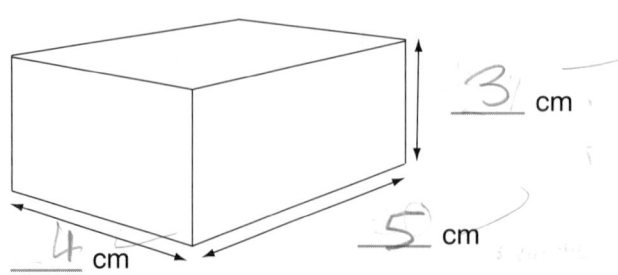

3 cm
5 cm
4 cm

94%

Paper 10

Look at these shapes.

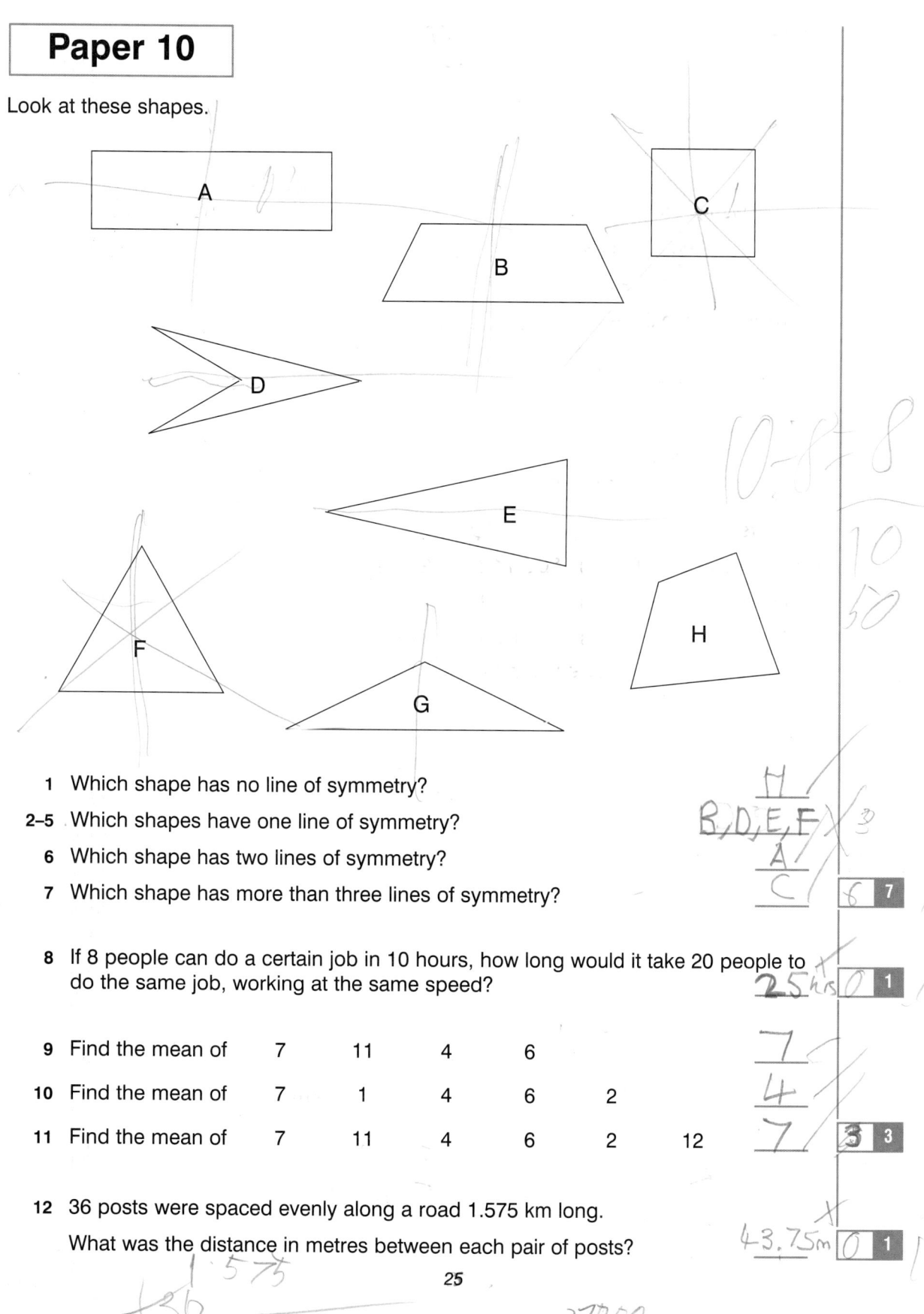

1. Which shape has no line of symmetry?
2–5. Which shapes have one line of symmetry?
6. Which shape has two lines of symmetry?
7. Which shape has more than three lines of symmetry?

8. If 8 people can do a certain job in 10 hours, how long would it take 20 people to do the same job, working at the same speed?

9. Find the mean of 7   11   4   6
10. Find the mean of 7   1   4   6   2
11. Find the mean of 7   11   4   6   2   12

12. 36 posts were spaced evenly along a road 1.575 km long.
    What was the distance in metres between each pair of posts?

25

13–19 Complete the following chart.

Wholesale price (Price at the factory)	Retail price (Price in the shop)	Profit (Money made by shopkeeper)
£7.85	£9.22	£1.37
£14.76	£17.10	£2.34
£38.75	£44.42	£5.67
£17.37	£21.14	£3.77
£41.85	£50.04	£8.19
£54.89	£67.76	£12.87
£0.87	£1.05	£0.18

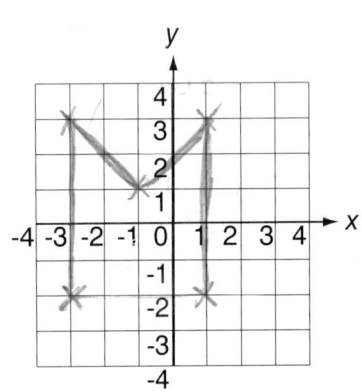

20–24 Plot the following co-ordinates on the chart and join them in the order you plot them.

(−3,−2)   (−3,3)   (−1,1)   (1,3)   (1,−2)

25 What letter have you made?   M

26–28 Emma (who is 8 years old), Richard (who is 7), and Katie (who is 5), share £10.00 in the ratio of their ages.

Emma gets ___5___, Richard gets ___3___ and Katie gets ___2___.

29 What must be added to 375 g to make 1 kg?   125 g

30 How many packets, each holding 125 g, can be filled from a case holding 3 kg?   12

Write these as fractions in their lowest terms.

31 3.8 $3\frac{4}{5}$

32 11.4 $11\frac{2}{5}$

33 11.002 $11\frac{1}{500}$

34 3.25 $3\frac{1}{4}$

35 6.5 $6\frac{5}{10}$

36 1.12 $1\frac{3}{25}$

26

Mr and Mrs Black took their three children from Norwich to Cromer by train.
The tickets for the five people totalled £31.50.
All the children travelled at half price.   6.3   3.15
37   How much was an adult ticket?   9.45   £11.05

	Train A	Train B	Train C	Train D
Norwich	06.15	07.33	20.48	22.10
Wroxham	06.26	07.48	20.32	21.54
Worstead	06.35	07.55	20.24	21.47
North Walsham	06.45	08.02	20.19	21.41
Gunton	06.51	08.08	20.09	21.35
Cromer	07.04	08.21	19.57	21.23

38   The fastest train for the Black family going to Cromer was train   B
39   The slowest train for the Black family returning to Norwich was train   C
40   If I leave Wroxham on the 7:48 train, and spend the day in Cromer,
     leaving on the 19:57 train, how long am I actually in Cromer?   12 hr   9 min
41   At what time does the 19:57 train from Cromer arrive in North Walsham?   20.19

I live in Norwich and travel to Cromer on the 06:15 train, returning home on the 21:23 train.

42   How long will I spend travelling on the train that day?   1 hr   36 min
43   At what time does the 20:09 from Gunton reach Wroxham?   20.32

44–50   In a sale all goods were reduced by 20%. Complete the chart below.

Ordinary price	Sale price
£20.00	£16
£35.00	£28
£60.00	£48
£180.00	£144
£55.00	£44
£40.00	£32
£275.00	£220

27

Paper 11

This graph represents the journeys of a cyclist and a motorist. The motorist is faster than the cyclist.

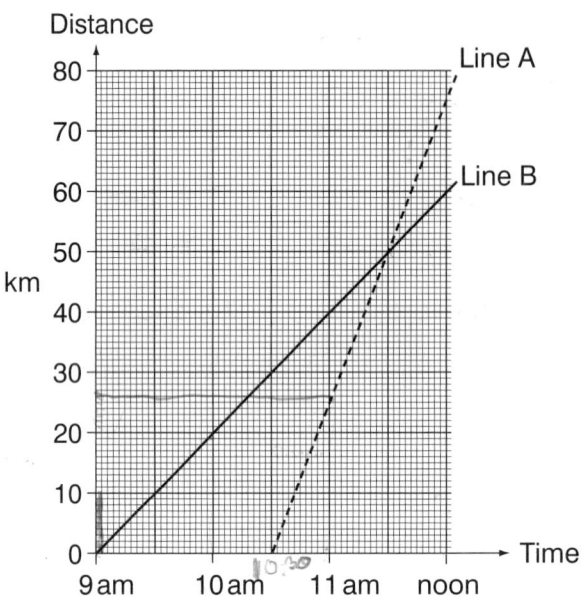

1. Which line represents the journey of the cyclist?   B
2. At what speed (km covered in 1 hr) was the cyclist travelling?   20 km/hr
3. At what speed was the motorist travelling?   27 km/hr
4. At what time did the motorist start his journey?   10:30 am
5. At what time did the cyclist start his journey?   9 am
6. At what time did the motorist overtake the cyclist?   11:30 am
7. How many km had the cyclist done when he was overtaken?   50 Km

8. What would be the approximate cost of 13 CDs at £4.98 each (to the nearest £)?   £7.00

9. The average of 4 numbers is $10\frac{1}{2}$.
   If the average of 3 of them is 9 what is the 4th number?   8

10–14 Arrange in order of size, putting the largest first.

$\frac{1}{2} \times 12$ $\frac{2}{3} \times 8$ $\frac{5}{6} \times 4$ $\frac{3}{8} \times 3$ $\frac{3}{4} \times 6$ 24

5/6   3/4   2/3   1/2   3/8

Some children in a Youth Club made this Venn diagram to show which type of music they prefer.

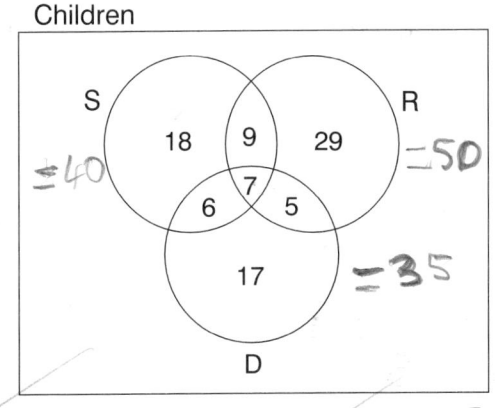

S = soul
R = rock
D = disco

15–17 40 children like soul, 50 like rock and 35 like disco music.

18 The number of children who like both soul and rock is   16
19 How many like soul and disco?   13
20 How many children like all three types of music?   7
21 How many children don't like soul?   51
22 How many don't like rock?   41
23 How many children don't like disco?   56
24 How many children were there altogether?   91   10

Underline the correct answer in each line.

25 $\frac{1}{8} + \frac{1}{4}$ = $\frac{1}{12}$ $\frac{2}{12}$ $\frac{3}{8}$ $\frac{1}{4}$
26 2.00 − 1.77 =   0.33   0.23   3.77   1.23
27 0.3 × 0.3 =   0.09   0.6   0.06   0.33
28 3 ÷ 0.6 =   0.2   0.5   0.18   5

0.6 1.2 1.8 2.4 3

29–33 Plot the points (1,3), (1,−1), (−3,−1) on the grid below.

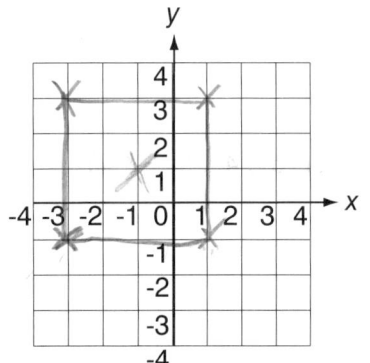

4   4

These points are the vertices of a rectangle. Mark the fourth vertex and draw the rectangle.

34–35 The co-ordinates of the fourth vertex are (−3, 3).

36–37 The co-ordinates of the centre of the square are (−1, 1).

Multiply each of the following by 100.

38 26.2   2620   **39** 8.9   890   **40** 25.16   2516

41–43 A cash box contains some coins to the value of £5.25.

There are twice as many 5p coins as 2p coins, and twice as many 2p coins as 1p coins.

This means there are:

£2 5p coins   £1 2p coins   50p 1p coins

44–46 The ages of Grandad, Uncle John and Tom add up to 105 years.

Grandad is twice as old as Uncle John, and Uncle John is twice as old as Tom.

Grandad is 60 years old, Uncle John is 30 years old and Tom is 15 years old.

Divide each of the following by 1000.

47 34.2   0.0342
48 8.6   0.0086
49 274.6   0.2746
50 3   0.003

Paper 12

1–5

34 | 43 | 52 | 61 | 70 ×10 −3 337 | 427 | 517 | 607 | 697

$5 \times 5 = 5^2$ $2 \times 2 \times 2 = 2^3$. Now write these in the same way.

6 $10 \times 10 \times 10 \times 10 =$ 10000
7 $7 \times 7 \times 7 =$ 363
8 $5 \times 5 \times 5 \times 5 \times 5 =$
9 $1 \times 1 \times 1 \times 1 \times 1 \times 1 =$
10 $4 \times 4 \times 4 \times 4 =$
11 $11 \times 11 \times 11 \times 11 \times 11 =$
12 What number is $1 \times 1 \times 1 \times 1 \times 1 \times 1$?

13 Find the area of a hall which is 9 metres long and 7 metres wide.
14 What is the perimeter of the hall?

At the supermarket there were various sizes of *Marvello*.

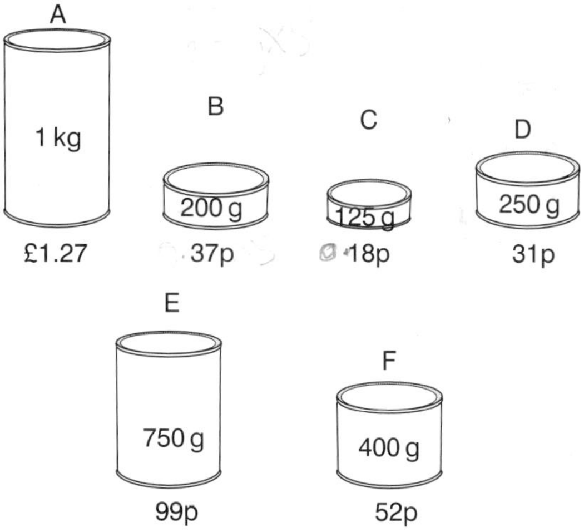

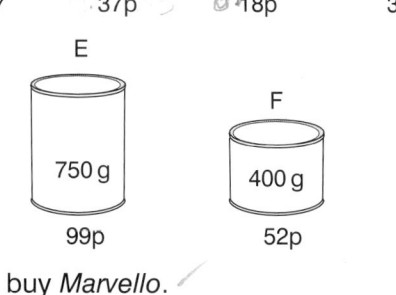

15 Tin ___ was the best bargain.
16 Tin ___ was the second best.
17 Tin ___ was the third best.
18 Tin ___ was the fourth best.
19 Tin ___ was the fifth best.
20 Tin ___ was the most expensive way to buy *Marvello*.

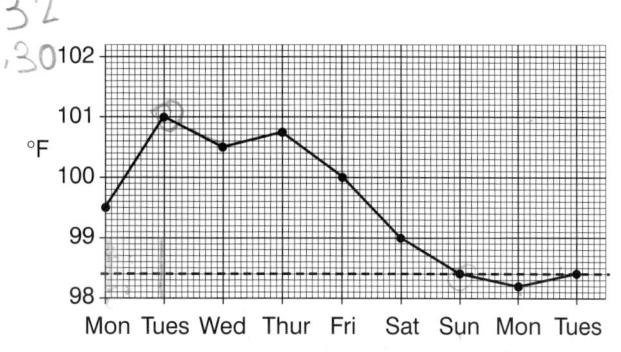

Here is Pete's temperature chart when he was ill.

The dotted line shows the normal temperature of a person.

21 On how many days was his temperature above normal?
22 On how many days was his temperature below normal?

31

23 On which day do you think he was most ill?
24 On which day do you think he started getting better?
25 What is a person's normal temperature?

In the end-of-term tests Zanna got the following marks.

Mathematics 54/75 English 48/60
History 27/40 French 25/40
Geography 39/50 Art 15/20

26 Her best subject was _Art_
27 2nd was _Geography_
28 3rd was _English_
29 4th was _History_
30 5th was _French_
31 6th was _Mathematics_

Write the next two amounts in each line.

32–33 12 13 15 18 22 27
34–35 5000 500 50 5 0.5 0.05
36–37 1 1½ 2½ 4 6 8½
38–39 0.6 0.7 0.8 0.9 1 1.1
40–41 0.125 0.250 0.375 0.500

Here are the scores in a mental arithmetic test out of 20.

Name	Peter	Cressida	Petra	Greg	Helen
Score	17	16	18	16	17

42–43 What are the **mode** scores?
44 What is the median?
45 What is the **range**?
46 What is the mean?

Peter's test was wrongly marked and he should have got 16 not 17.

47 What is the mode score now?
48 What is the median now?
49 What is the range now?
50 What is the mean now?

Paper 13

1–3 Complete the figures below. The dotted line is the line of symmetry.

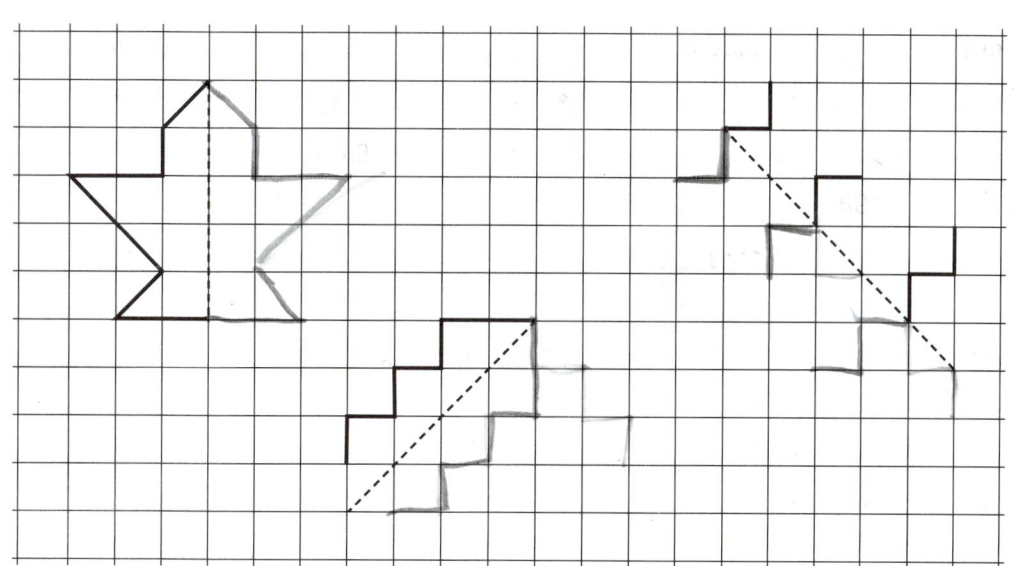

Underline the correct answer in each line.

4	$\frac{1}{5} + \frac{2}{10}$	=	$\frac{3}{15}$	$\frac{2}{5}$	$\frac{3}{10}$	$\frac{5}{10}$	$\frac{1}{5}$
5	$0.49 \div 7$	=	7	0.7	0.07	70	700
6	20% of 35	=	7	8	15	20	25
7	$4^2 - 3^2$	=	1	2	3	7	9
8	$2^3 - 2^2$	=	1	2	3	4	5
9	25% of 1 metre	=	1 cm	2 cm	10 cm	25 cm	25 m
10	$0.1 \times 0.1 \times 0.1$	=	0.3	0.2	0.001	0.003	0.0001
11	$\frac{1}{3} + \frac{1}{6}$	=	$\frac{2}{3}$	$\frac{1}{2}$	$\frac{1}{9}$	$\frac{2}{9}$	$\frac{1}{18}$

12–14 Share £3.40 among Angela, Ben and Claire. For every 10p Angela gets, Ben gets 5p, and Claire gets 2p.

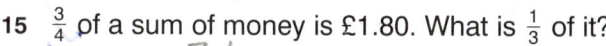

Angela gets _____, Ben gets _____ and Claire gets _____

15 $\frac{3}{4}$ of a sum of money is £1.80. What is $\frac{1}{3}$ of it?

16 Multiply 3.7 by itself, and then take 3.7 from the answer.

17 Add together 3.7, 2.95 and 0.187.

18 Take 1.689 from 3.2.

19 Divide 799 by 17.

33

Multiply each of the numbers below by 1000.

20 2.75

21 38.2

22 0.125

23 0.875

The bar chart below shows the marks in Mathematics for Class 8.

The maximum mark was 100.
One boy gained over 90.

$\frac{2}{5}$ of those who received between 81 and 90 were girls.

$\frac{3}{4}$ of those who received between 71 and 80 were boys.

$\frac{1}{2}$ of those who received between 61 and 70 were girls.

$\frac{1}{3}$ of those who received between 51 and 60 were girls.

$\frac{1}{2}$ of those who received between 41 and 50 were boys.

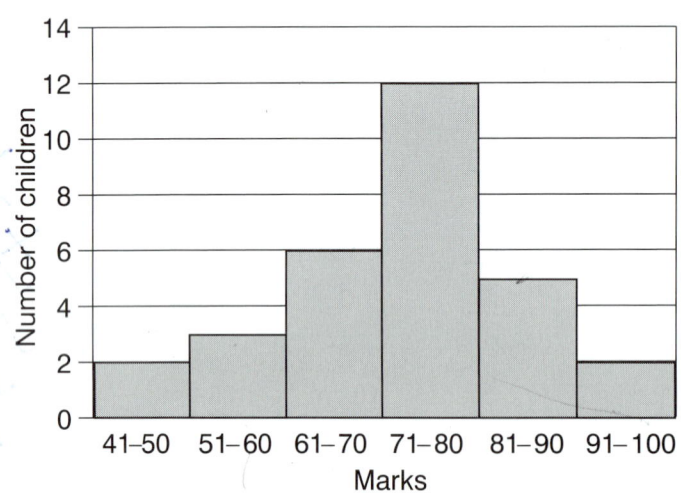

24 How many children took the test?
25 How many girls got over 90 marks?
26 How many boys received between 61 and 70 marks?
27 How many girls received between 41 and 50 marks?
28 In the 81 to 90 mark range how many were boys?
29 In the 71 to 80 mark range how many were girls?
30 How many boys received between 51 and 60 marks?

31–40 Fill in the multiplication table.

×	5	4	9	2
2	10	8	18	4
3	15	12	27	6
7	35	28	63	14
1	5	4	9	2

41–46 Fill in the missing numbers.

$\frac{4}{5} \times \frac{5}{5} = \frac{20}{25}$ $\frac{7}{11} \times \frac{11}{11} = \frac{77}{121}$ $\frac{7}{8} \times \frac{8}{8} = \frac{56}{64}$

$\frac{2}{7} \times \frac{6}{6} = \frac{12}{42}$ $\frac{3}{4} \times \frac{12}{12} = \frac{36}{48}$ $\frac{7}{9} \times \frac{7}{7} = \frac{49}{63}$

47 If 13 articles cost £1.56 what would 7 articles cost?   £0.84

48–50 Share 39 sweets among Penny, Polly and Prue giving Penny 3 times as much as Polly, and Polly 3 times as much as Prue.

Penny has 27, Polly has 9 and Prue has 3.

27 9 3

96%

Paper 14

1–3 Complete this table.

60	144	72	132	120
5	12	6	11	10

4   £ 0.38
     × 11
     ‾‾‾‾
     84.18

5   £0.57
    9)5.13

6   1030
   − 752
     ‾‾‾‾
      278

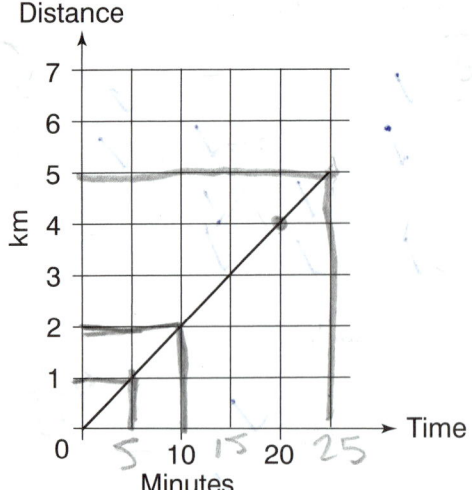

Look at the line graph and then answer these questions.

7   I'll do 2 km in __10__ min.

8   I'll do 1 km in __5__ min.

9   How far will I travel in 25 minutes?   __5 km__

10 What is my speed in km/h?   __20 km/h__

11 What number when multiplied by 25 gives the same answer as 45 × 40?   __72__

Solve these equations.

12 $3 + a = 15$
    $a = 12$

13 $x + 4 = 7$
    $x = 3$

14 $5 + a = 7$
    $a = 2$

15 $y - 7 = 9$
    $y = 16$

16 $b - 4 = 8$
    $b = 12$

17 $c - 1 = 5$
    $c = 6$

18–21 Do these divisions.

   128   131   132   129
 7)896   6)786   9)1188   4)516

22 Draw a circle around the division with the largest quotient.

It takes me 19 minutes to walk home from school.

23 If I leave school at 3:45 p.m. what time will I get home?   __4:04 pm__

24 How many minutes are there from 10:29 p.m. Monday to 2:05 a.m. Tuesday?   __216__ min

36

4 schools in Sandville made these pie charts which show how many of their pupils walk to school.

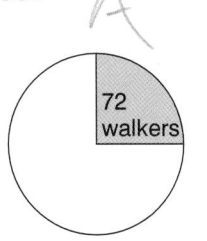

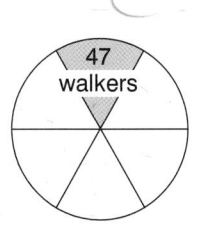

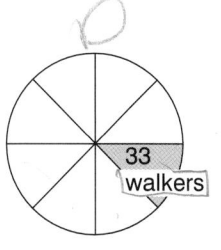

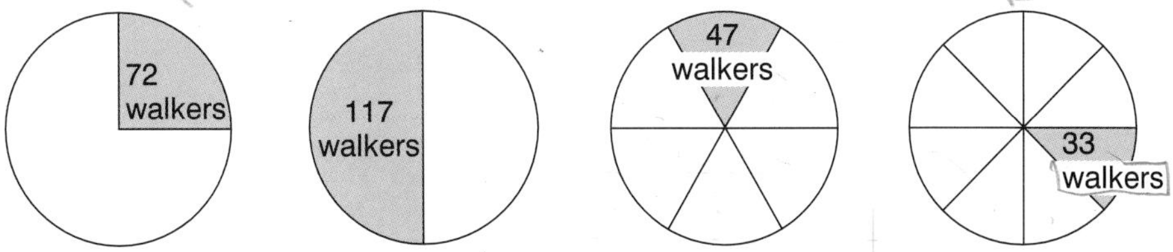

A: 72 walkers
B: 117 walkers
C: 47 walkers
D: 33 walkers

Write the total number of pupils in each school.

25 School A 288
26 School B 234
27 School C 182 ✗
28 School D 132 ✗

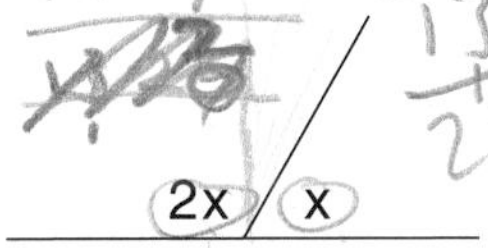

29 Angle x = 85° 60
30 Angle 2x = 95° 120

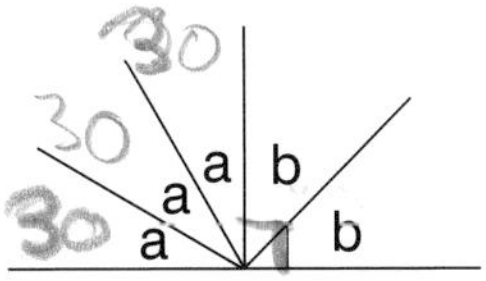

31 Angle a = 30°
32 Angle b = 45°

Complete the timetable below.

33–43 There are 5 40-minute lessons, with a break of 15 minutes after the second lesson.

	Begins	Ends
1st lesson	9:10 ✗	9:55
2nd lesson	9:55	10:35
Break	10:35	10:50
3rd lesson	10:50	11:30
4th lesson	11:30	12:10
5th lesson	12:10	12:50

37

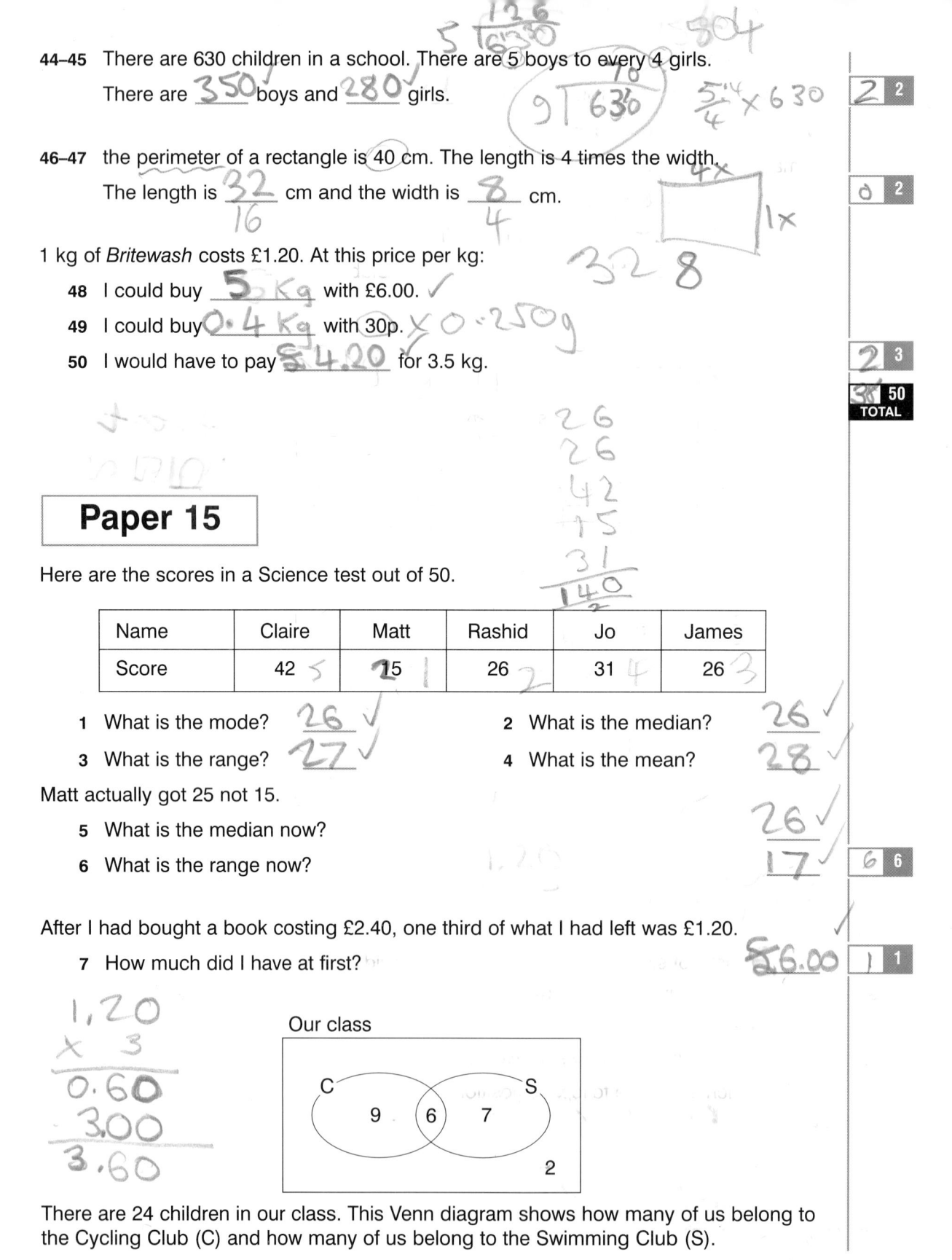

44–45 There are 630 children in a school. There are 5 boys to every 4 girls.
There are __350__ boys and __280__ girls.

46–47 the perimeter of a rectangle is 40 cm. The length is 4 times the width.
The length is __32__ cm and the width is __8__ cm.

1 kg of *Britewash* costs £1.20. At this price per kg:

48 I could buy __5 Kg__ with £6.00.

49 I could buy __0.4 Kg__ with 30p.

50 I would have to pay __£4.20__ for 3.5 kg.

Paper 15

Here are the scores in a Science test out of 50.

Name	Claire	Matt	Rashid	Jo	James
Score	42	15	26	31	26

1. What is the mode? __26__
2. What is the median? __26__
3. What is the range? __27__
4. What is the mean? __28__

Matt actually got 25 not 15.

5. What is the median now? __26__
6. What is the range now? __17__

After I had bought a book costing £2.40, one third of what I had left was £1.20.

7. How much did I have at first? __£6.00__

Our class

There are 24 children in our class. This Venn diagram shows how many of us belong to the Cycling Club (C) and how many of us belong to the Swimming Club (S).

8 How many belong to the Cycling Club? __15__
9 How many belong to the Swimming Club? __13__
10 How many belong to both clubs ? __6__
11 How many belong to neither club? __2__
12 How many belong to one club only ? __16__
13 How many children don't belong to the Cycling Club? __9__
14 How many children don't belong to the Swimming Club? __11__

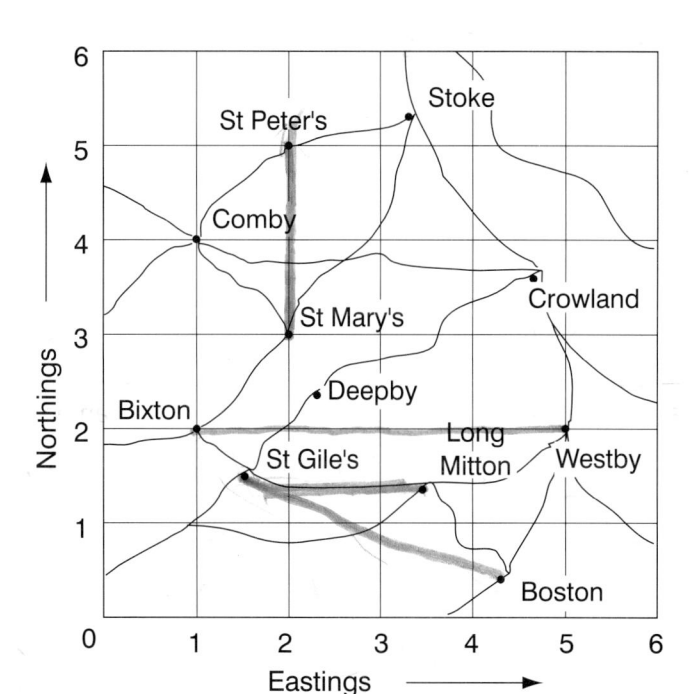

This map is covered with a grid, the lines of which are numbered 0–6 for eastings and 0–6 for northings. The position of towns is found by giving their co-ordinates, e.g. Bixton is (1,2).

Some of the towns are not situated on the lines, but are inside the squares.

When this is so, the co-ordinates of the bottom left-hand corner of the square are given, e.g. Deepby is (2,2).

Scale: A side of a small square represents 10 km.

Name the towns which are at the following positions.

15 (2,5) __St Peter's__
16 (2,3) __St Mary's__
17 (3,1) __Long Mitton__
18 (4,0) __Boston__

39

Give the co-ordinates for the following towns.

19–20 Crowland (4, 3)
21–22 Westby (5, 2)
23–24 Comby (1, 4)
25–26 Stoke (3, 5)

Approximately, how far is it, as the crow flies (in a straight line), from:

27 St Giles to Long Mitton? 20 km
28 St Peter's to St Mary's? 20 km
29 St Giles to Boston? 30 km
30 Bixton to Westby? 40 km

31 Put a circle around the prime number.

20   21   22   (23)   24   25

There are 364 children in a school. There are 18 more girls than boys.

32 There are 191 girls.
33 There are 173 boys.

34 Take eleven from eleven thousand. 10989

35–38 Complete the following table.

	Length	Width	Area	Perimeter
Rectangle 1	7 m	4 m	28 m²	22 m
Rectangle 2	9 m	4 m	36 m²	26 m

Write the next two numbers in each line.

39–40   2 5 11 20 32 47 66
41–42   5.7 5.8 6.0 6.3 6.4 6.9
43–44   1½ 2¼ 2¾ 3¾ 5½ 7½
45–46   0.001 0.01 0.1 1 10
47–48   97 86 76 67 59 52
49–50   ¼ ⅜ ½ ⅝ ¾

Paper 16

Here is a pie chart which shows how many computers pupils in class 6C have at home.

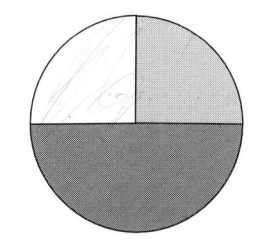

- No computer
- One computer
- More than one computer

1. What percentage of pupils have at least one computer at home?
2. What fraction of pupils have more than one computer at home?

If there are 32 pupils in class 6C:

3. How many do not have a computer at home?
4. How many have at least one computer at home?

5. Find the smallest number which must be added to 890 to make it exactly divisible by 31.

6. Find the sum of 47, 48 and 49.
7. Find the mean of 47, 48 and 49.
8. Find the range of 47, 48 and 49.

Our school swimming pool, which is 50 m long and 20 m wide, has a path 10 m wide all around it.

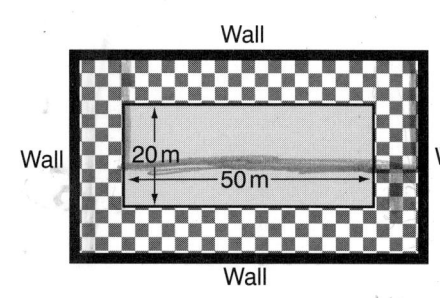

9. What is the area of the swimming pool?
10. What is the area of the whole complex (swimming pool and the path)?
11. What is the area of the path?
12. What is the perimeter of the swimming pool?
13. What is the total length of the wall?

14 Jenny bought 7 metres of material. She gave the assistant £20.00 and received £2.57 change.
What was the price of the material per metre? **£2.49**

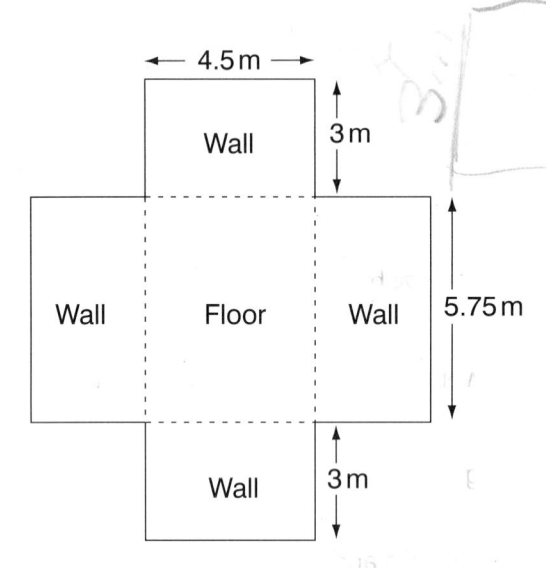

Here is a net of a model of a room, showing the walls and the floor.

```
         ← 4.5 m →
         ┌────────┐
         │  Wall  │ 3 m
         │        │
┌────────┼────────┼────────┐
│  Wall  │  Floor │  Wall  │ 5.75 m
│        │        │        │
└────────┼────────┼────────┘
         │  Wall  │ 3 m
         └────────┘
```

15 How high is the room? **3 m**
16 What is the total area of the walls? **61.5 m²**

17 4 × ✱ = 8 + 20
    ✱ = **7**

18 ✈ ÷ 2 = 10 + 12
    ✈ = **44**

19 10 − ✱ = 27 ÷ 3
    ✱ = **1**

20 3 + ✈ = 20 − 3
    ✈ = **14**

Divide each number by 1000.
21 34.2   **0.0342**
22 8.6   **0.0086**
23 274.6 **0.2746**
24 3   **0.003**

Tim, Carl and Lewis together had 126 game cards. Carl won 3 from Tim, and Lewis lost 2 to Carl.
They then found that Tim had twice as many as Carl, and Carl had twice as many as Lewis.
25–27 At the end of the game Tim had **72**, Carl **36** and Lewis **18**.
28–30 At the start of the game Tim had **75**, Carl **31** and Lewis **20**.

We asked 144 children at our school how they spent their holiday.
When we got their answers we made this pie chart.

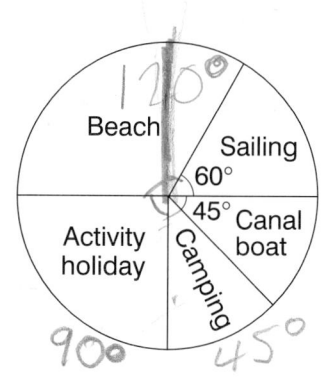

Beach 120°
Sailing 60°
Canal boat 45°
Camping 45°
Activity holiday 90°

31 How many children went to the beach?
32 How many went sailing?
33 The number of children who went on an activities holiday was
34 How many went camping?
35 How many went canal boating?

In a school there were altogether 476 pupils and teachers.
The girls + the teachers = 241
The boys + the teachers = 258
36–38 There were 23 teachers, 235 boys and 218 girls.

Underline the correct answer in each line.

39	$\frac{1}{3} + \frac{1}{6}$	=	$\frac{2}{3}$	$\frac{1}{2}$	$\frac{1}{9}$	$\frac{2}{9}$	$\frac{1}{6}$
40	$\frac{1}{5} + \frac{7}{10}$	=	$\frac{8}{10}$	$\frac{8}{15}$	$\frac{9}{15}$	$\frac{11}{15}$	$\frac{9}{10}$
41	111 − 19	=	100	128	102	82	92
42	6 ÷ 1.2	=	48	5	50	0.5	5.3
43	$3^3 - 5^2$	=	8	15	3	2	1
44	60 ÷ 3	=	4	8	20	32	57
45	25% of 48	=	12	24	25	48	60
46	$\frac{1}{4} \times \frac{1}{4}$	=	1	$\frac{1}{8}$	$\frac{1}{16}$	$\frac{1}{2}$	$\frac{1}{6}$

47–48 Put a circle around the prime numbers.

13   14   15   16   17

49–50 Underline the prime factors of 18.

2   3   4   5   6   7   8

Paper 17

1–5 Here are Ben's exam marks. Change them into percentages.

Subject	Actual mark	Possible mark	Percentage
Science	12	15	80
French	21	35	60
English	68	80	85
Art	63	70	90
Music	14	20	70

6 Ben's total mark in Science and French was __33__ out of 50.

7 His average percentage mark in Science and French was __66%__

8–12 Write down Peter's actual marks.

Subject	Actual mark	Possible mark	Percentage
Science	9	15	60
French	28	35	80
English	44	80	55
Art	49	70	70
Music	13	20	65

13 Peter's total mark in English and Art was __93__ out of 150.

14 His average percentage mark in English and Art was __62%__

Write each of these numbers to the nearest whole number.

15 8.35   __8__   16 0.71   __1__

17 4.48   __4__   18 0.123   __0__

19–21 There are 56 beads. Sam has twice as many as Ren, who has twice as many as Aisha.

Sam has __32__ beads, Ren has __16__ beads and Aisha has __8__ beads.

44

These are the nets of solids. What solids will they make? Choose from: **square based pyramid**, **triangular based pyramid**, **triangular prism**, **pentagonal prism**, **cube**, **cuboid**, **sphere** or **cone**. (You may not need all the answer lines)

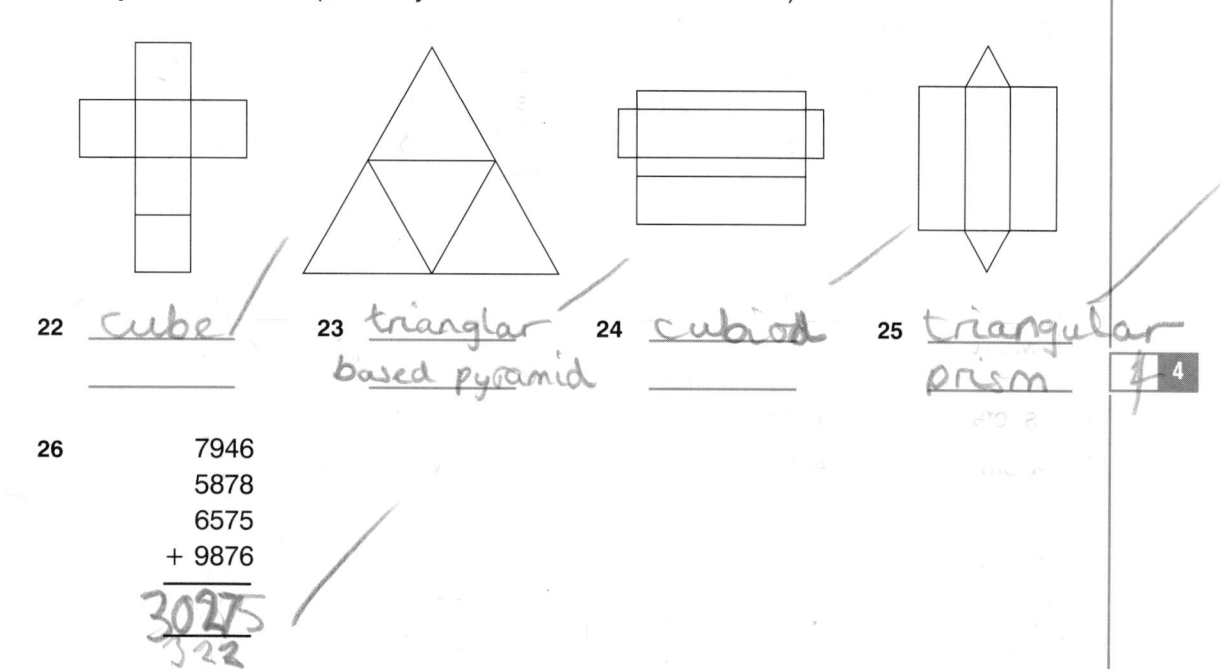

22 cube   23 trianglar based pyramid   24 cubiod   25 triangular prism

26
```
   7946
   5878
   6575
 + 9876
  ─────
  30275
```

27 Write the answer to the last sum in words.
thiry thousand, two hudred and seventy five.

28–37 Complete the following chart.

	Length	Width	Perimeter	Area
Rectangle 1	29 m	1 m	60 m	29 m²
Rectangle 2	28 m	2 m	60 m	56 m²
Rectangle 3	25 m	5 m	60 m	125 m²
Rectangle 4	20 m	10 m	60 m	200 m²
Rectangle 5	15 m	15 m	60 m	225 m²

38 Multiply 0.0908 by 25.   2.27

39–41 Convert this recipe for pasta from imperial to metric units (to the nearest 5 g).

Ingredient	Imperial	Metric
plain flour	5 oz	25 g
semolina flour	12 oz	60 g
eggs	11 eggs	55 g

45

42–45 Ounces or grammes are a good unit for measuring flour in the pasta recipe on page 45.

Give the most appropriate metric unit to measure:

the distance from Earth to the Sun.   km

the amount of petrol in a car.   l

the weight of a train.   kg

the thickness of this book.   cm

46–50 Put in order, smallest first.

0.707   0.78   0.708   0.7   0.77

Paper 18

1 In a class, 19 children have dogs and 18 children have cats.

If 15 children have both dogs and cats find the smallest possible number of children in the class.

2 How many times can 27 be subtracted from 1431?

3 12 toys were bought for £1.25 each and sold for £1.60 each.

What was the total profit?

4–15 Here are some exchange rates.

£1	=	1.46 US Dollars
£1	=	119 Kenyan Shillings
£1	=	1.42 Euros
£1	=	2.13 Australian Dollars

Complete the table.

£	US Dollars	Kenyan Shillings	Euros	Australian Dollars
£10.00				
£5.00				
£0.50				

16–19 Arrange these numbers in order, putting the largest first.

7.800   7.088   7.880   7.008

7.88   7.8   7.088   7.008

20–25 Complete the following table.

Fraction	Decimal	Percentage
½	0.5	50%
1/4	0.25	25%
⅕	0.2	20%

26–30 Solve these equations.

$\frac{56}{a} = 8$ $\frac{49}{b} = 7$ $\frac{72}{9} = x$ $\frac{y}{4} = 3$ $\frac{z}{9} = 7$

a = 7   b = 7   x = 8   y = 12   z = 63

31 The product of two numbers is 111.
The largest number is 37. What is the other number?   3

	Train A	Train B	Train C	Train D
Westbury	08.11	09.20	18.09	20.09
Trowbridge	08.19	09.30	17.58	20.04
Bath	08.45	09.54	17.23	19.31
Bristol	09.00	10.11	17.05	19.17

32 Which is the fastest of these trains?   A

33 How long does the fastest train take to travel from Westbury to Bristol?   49 mins

34 Which is the slowest of these trains?   C

35 How long does the slowest train take to do the entire journey?   1 hr 4 mins

36 If I live in Westbury, and want to be in Bath before 9 a.m., on which train must I travel?   A

37 How long does the 19:31 from Bath take to travel to Westbury?   38 mins

38 When should the 17:23 from Bath arrive in Westbury?   18:09

47

Using this world time chart answer the following.

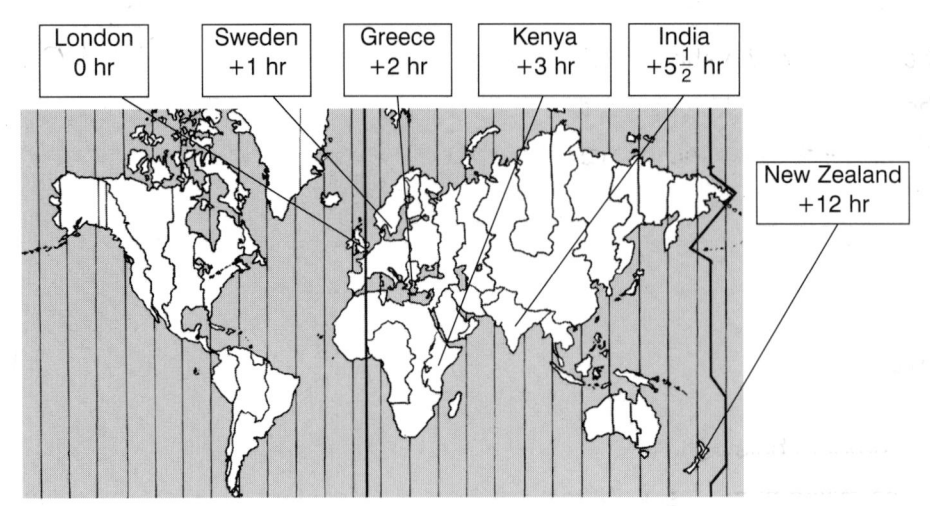

Location	Offset
London	0 hr
Sweden	+1 hr
Greece	+2 hr
Kenya	+3 hr
India	+5½ hr
New Zealand	+12 hr

39 When it is 10:00 a.m. in London what time is it New Zealand? 10:00pm

40 When it is 9:00 a.m. in London what time is it India? 1:30pm

41 When it is 3:30 p.m. in Greece what time is it London? 1:30pm

42 When it is 1:15 p.m. in Sweden what time is it London? 12:15pm

43 If I made a telephone call from Kenya to India at 3:00 p.m., what time would it be in India? 5:30pm

	Years	Months
Tony is	10	8
Claire is	9	6
Simon is	11	4
Mandy is	10	2

44 Look at the table. The children's ages add up to 40 years 80 months

45–46 What is the mean age of the four children? 10 years 5 months

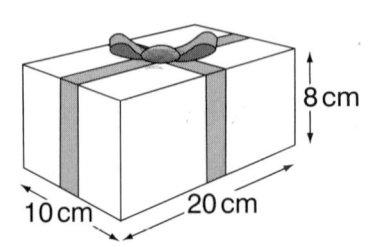

Here is a box 20 cm long, 10 cm wide, and 8 cm high.

48

A ribbon is placed round the box, once lengthwise, and once round the width.

47 What is the perimeter of a long side? 40 cm
48 What is the perimeter of a short side? 20 cm
49 What is the perimeter of the base of the box? 60 cm
50 If I allow 35 cm for the bow, how much ribbon will I need? 85 cm

Paper 19

Divide each of the numbers below by 10.
Give your answers as mixed numbers, with fractions in their lowest terms.

1 78 $7\frac{4}{5}$
2 475 $47\frac{1}{2}$
3 312.5 $31\frac{1}{4}$
4 1.25 $1\frac{1}{8}$

5 How many metres must be added to 1.35 km to make 4 km? 2.65 m

6–13 Fill in the multiplication grid.

×	5	7	2	3
3	15	21	6	9
8	40	56	16	24
4	20	28	8	12
9	45	63	18	27

Give the answers to the following in decimal form.

14 17 tenths   0.17
15 143 hundredths   0.0143
16 47 units   47.0
17 7 thousandths   0.007
18 259 tens   259.0
19 14 hundredths   0.014

Insert signs to make the following correct.

20–22 5 × 5 − 1 = 13 + 12
23–25 (7 − 4) − 2 = 25 ÷ 25

Insert the missing numbers in these.

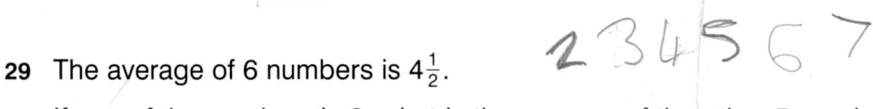

26 4.9 × __100__ = 490
27 __1.23__ ÷ 10 = 0.123
28 0.136 × 100 = __13.6__

29 The average of 6 numbers is $4\frac{1}{2}$.
If one of the numbers is 2, what is the average of the other 5 numbers? __5__

30–35 VAT (Value Added Tax) is added to the price of some goods. It is charged at $17\frac{1}{2}$% (£17.50 on each £100). Complete the following table.

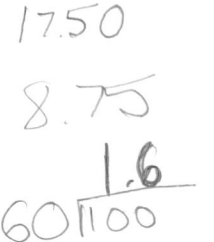

Price before VAT	VAT	Total price
£300	£52.50	£352.50
£150	£26.25	£176.25
£60	£29.16	£89.16

36–41 Three rectangular pieces of card have the same area (24 cm²). Fill in the other measurements.

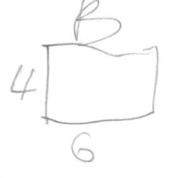

	Length	Width	Perimeter	Area
Piece A	8 cm	__3__ cm	__22__ cm	24 cm²
Piece B	__6__ cm	4 cm	__20__ cm	24 cm²
Piece C	12 cm	__2__ cm	__28__ cm	24 cm²

What percentages are the following fractions?

42 $\frac{15}{30}$ = __50__%   43 $\frac{4}{25}$ = __16__%

Look at the diagram. Answer the following questions below by writing YES or NO. It would help you if you drew in the diagonals with a ruler.

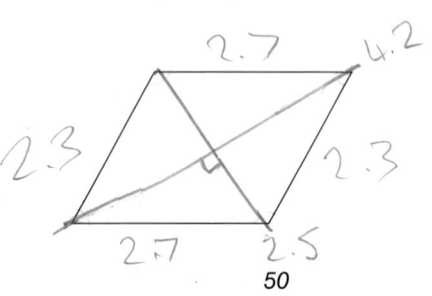

44 Are all the sides the same length?

45 Are the opposite sides parallel?

46 Are all the angles equal?

47 Are the diagonals the same length?

48 Do the diagonals cross at right angles?

49 Is this a rhombus?

50 Is this a parallelogram?

Paper 20

The cost of some rides in the *Space Adventure Park* are:

| Galaxy | £1.65 | Laser | £2.80 |
| Big Wheel | £1.45 | Spaceship | £2.70 |

Amy went on two rides. She had £4.50 change from £10.

1–2 Which two rides did she go on? _____ and _____

John also went on two rides. He had £5.65 change from £10.

3–4 Which two rides did he go on? _____ and _____

5 How much would it cost to go on all four rides? _____

6 What is the mean price of a ride? _____

7 In the library there are 200 books. 58 of them are non-fiction.
   What percentage of the books are non-fiction? _____

8–10 In Little Marsden the population is 17 222.

   The men and women together number 9142 and the women and children together number 13 201.

   There are _____ women, _____ men and _____ children.

11 Take five hundred and sixty-seven from one thousand. Write out your answer in figures. _____

Complete the figures below. The dotted line is the line of symmetry.

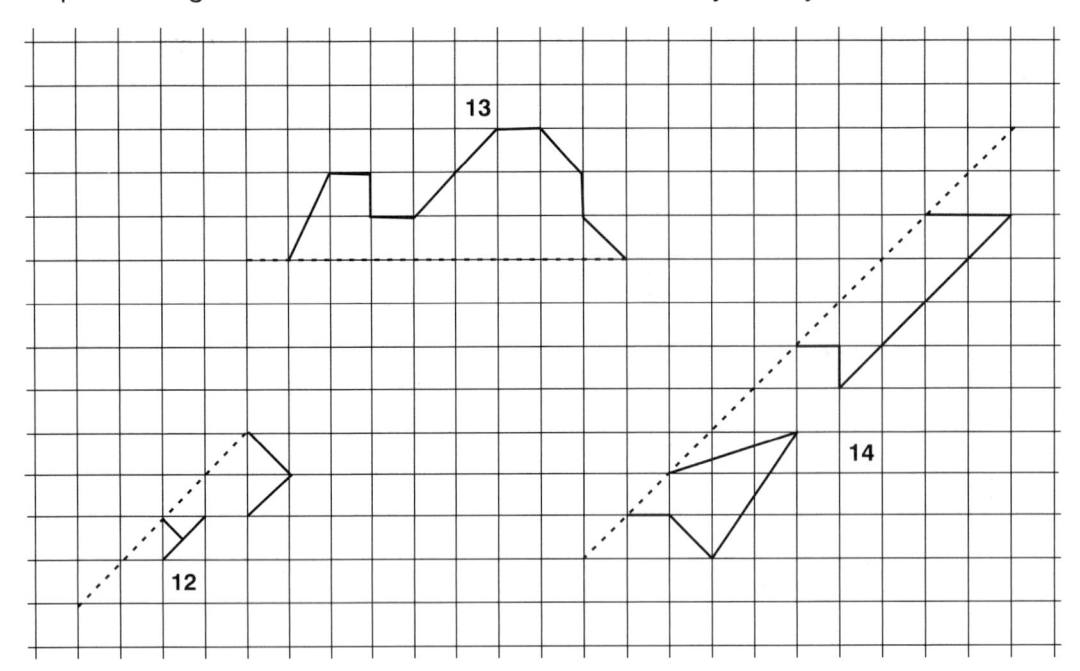

If the big hand of a clock is at 12 and the small hand is not, what time is it when the angle between the two hands is:

15 180° _____ o'clock
16 30° _____ o'clock
17 120° _____ o'clock
18 60° _____ o'clock
19 150° _____ o'clock
20 90° _____ o'clock

21 John multiplied a number by 9 instead of dividing it by 9.
    His answer was 4131. What should his answer have been? _____

22 20% of my money is £2.55.
    What is $\frac{2}{5}$ of it? _____

23 What amount must be added to 178.5 g to make 1 kg? _____ g

Put a ring around the correct answers in each line.

24 13 × 11 =   132   143   133
25 15² =   165   155   225
26 64   =   8²   9²   7²
27 702 ÷ 3 =   214   234   204
28 14 × 12 =   154   148   168

52

Plot these points and join them in order.

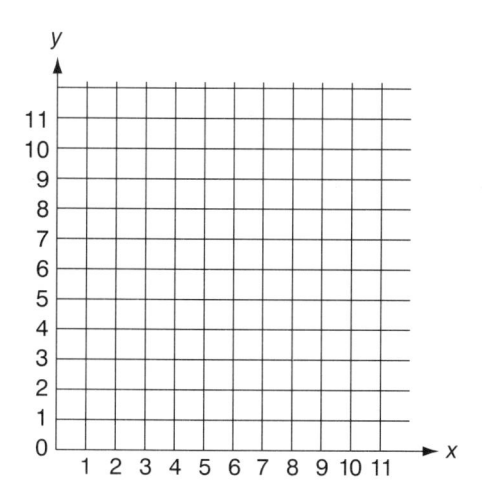

29–41 (5,1) (5,5) (2,3) (5,6) (2,5) (4,7) (6,11) (8,7) (10,5) (7,6) (10,3) (7,5) (7,1)

42 What have you drawn? _____

The three largest oceans in the world cover the following areas.

Ocean	Square km	Square miles
Atlantic	82 217 000	31 736 000
Indian	73 481 000	28 364 000
Pacific	165 384 000	63 838 000

Write the answers to the following questions in the table below.

43–44 Round the areas of the Atlantic Ocean to the nearest 100 000.

45–46 Round the areas of the Indian Ocean to the nearest 10 000.

47–48 Round the areas of the Pacific Ocean to the nearest 1 000 000.

Ocean	Square km	Square miles
Atlantic		
Indian		
Pacific		

Last Friday $\frac{1}{8}$ of the pupils in our school were absent.

There are 560 pupils altogether in the school.

49–50 There were _____ pupils absent and _____ pupils present.

Paper 21

The answers to the following product sums are either odd or even. Answer each question as either ODD or EVEN.

1. 84 × 36 is an _____ number
2. 163 × 297 is an _____ number
3. 729 × 1468 is an _____ number
4. 292 × 36 × 52 is an _____ number

Write the following amounts correct to the nearest £1.00.

5. £2.42 _____
6. £2.71 _____
7. £4.59 _____
8. £6.49 _____
9. £7.50 _____

$\frac{2}{3}$ rds of a sum of money is 48p.

10. What is $\frac{5}{8}$ ths of the sum of money? _____

Roast chicken must be cooked for 50 minutes per kg and then for an extra 20 minutes.

11–16 Complete this table of cooking times in hours and minutes.

Weight of chicken (kg)	Cooking time
1	____ hr ____ min
1.5	____ hr ____ min
2	____ hr ____ min
2.5	____ hr ____ min
3	____ hr ____ min
3.5	____ hr ____ min

Divide these numbers by 1000.

17. 374 _____
18. 14.8 _____
19. 2.55 _____

There are 420 children in a school. 45% of the pupils are boys.

20. How many boys are there? _____
21. How many girls are there? _____

£9.00 is shared between Paddy, Phil and Andy in the ratio of 8:5:2.

22. Paddy receives _____
23. Phil receives _____
24. Andy receives _____

25–29 Arrange in order, largest first.

$\frac{7}{12}$ $\frac{3}{8}$ $\frac{3}{4}$ $\frac{11}{24}$ $\frac{5}{6}$

_____   _____   _____   _____   _____

Suggest the best imperial unit to measure:

30 the distance from London to New York.

31 the amount of water in a jug.

32 the weight of a pencil.

33 the height of a man.

Convert these 24-hour clock times into a.m. and p.m.

(20:20)   (08:05)   (00:10)   (17:45)

34 _____   **35** _____   **36** _____   **37** _____

38–39 Add these children's ages.

	Years	Months
Zoe	10	11
Simon	10	8
David	11	4
Rachel	10	2
Tariq	10	8
Total	_____	_____

40–41 What is their average age?   _____ years   _____ months

Add the greatest to the smallest.

42   £$\frac{1}{2}$ £0.55   27 × 2p   £$\frac{13}{25}$ £1.00 – 49p   _____

43–45 Scott has $\frac{1}{3}$ as many computer games as Mike, and Mike has $\frac{1}{2}$ as many games as Nick.

Together they have 140 games.

Scott has _____ games, Mike has _____ games and Nick has _____ games.

We asked 72 children to name their favourite colour.
We made this pie chart.

- Blue 165°
- Orange
- Green
- Yellow
- 30°
- Red
- Pink

46 How many children prefer green?

47 How many children prefer blue?

48 How many prefer orange?

49 How many like red best?

50 The number of children who prefer pink is?

Paper 22

The school hall is 4 times as long as it is wide.

1 If the perimeter is 55 m, what is the length?

2 What is the width?

Ahmed has 30 sweets; 60% of them are toffees and the rest are chocolates.

Ben has 40 sweets; $\frac{3}{8}$ of them are chocolates and the rest are toffees.

3 Who has the most toffees?

4–5 How many more than _____ did he have?

6 Who had the most chocolates?

7–8 He had _____ more than _____ .

Here are the number of music CDs these 6 friends had.

Name	Pete	Lucy	Kath	Jez	Helen	Simone
Number	8	5	14	19	14	12

9 What is the mode? _____

10 What is the median? _____

11 What is the range? _____

12 What is the mean? _____

56

Give the value of the 7 in each of the following numbers.

13 13.78 _____   **14** 37.89 _____   **15** 378.95 _____

1432 + 798 = 2230 so:

16 3432 + 798 will be _____   **17** 2432 + 1798 will be _____

18 4432 + 798 will be _____

Fill in the next two numbers in each line.

19–20	95	89	84	80	___	___
21–22	89	77	67	59	___	___
23–24	31	33	36	40	___	___
25–26	144	121	100	81	___	___

27–32 On the squared paper, draw a bar chart to show the following information.

The number of cups of coffee sold at Buttercup Café last week:

Monday	90	Tuesday	110
Wednesday	70	Thursday	100
Friday	120	Saturday	140

Be careful to use a scale which will show this information accurately.

Write in your scale.

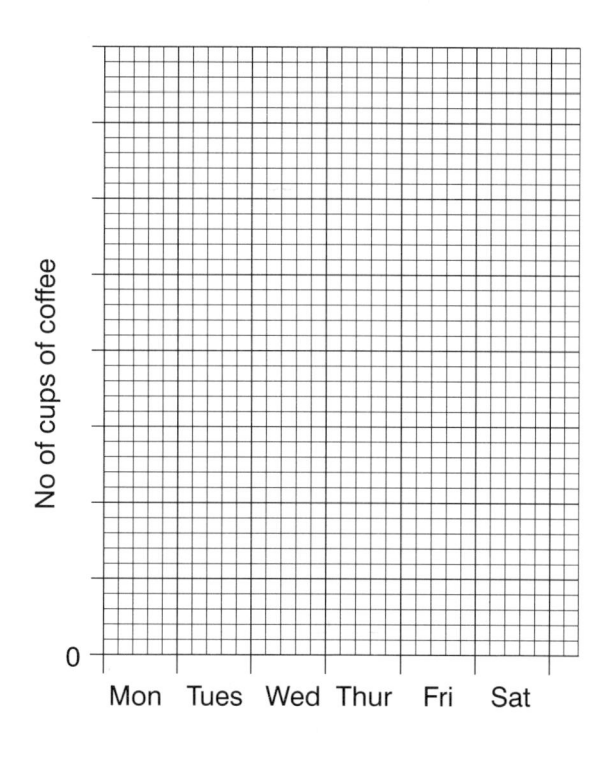

33–37 Here is part of a railway timetable. Fill in the times at which train B will reach the stations. It takes exactly the same time to do the journey as train A.

	Train A arrives at	Train B arrives at
Barwich	07.30	10.05
Hoole	07.48	_____
Carby	08.02	_____
Manton	08.15	_____
Pemby	08.29	_____
Durwich	08.54	_____

At the supermarket there were various sizes of *Disho*.

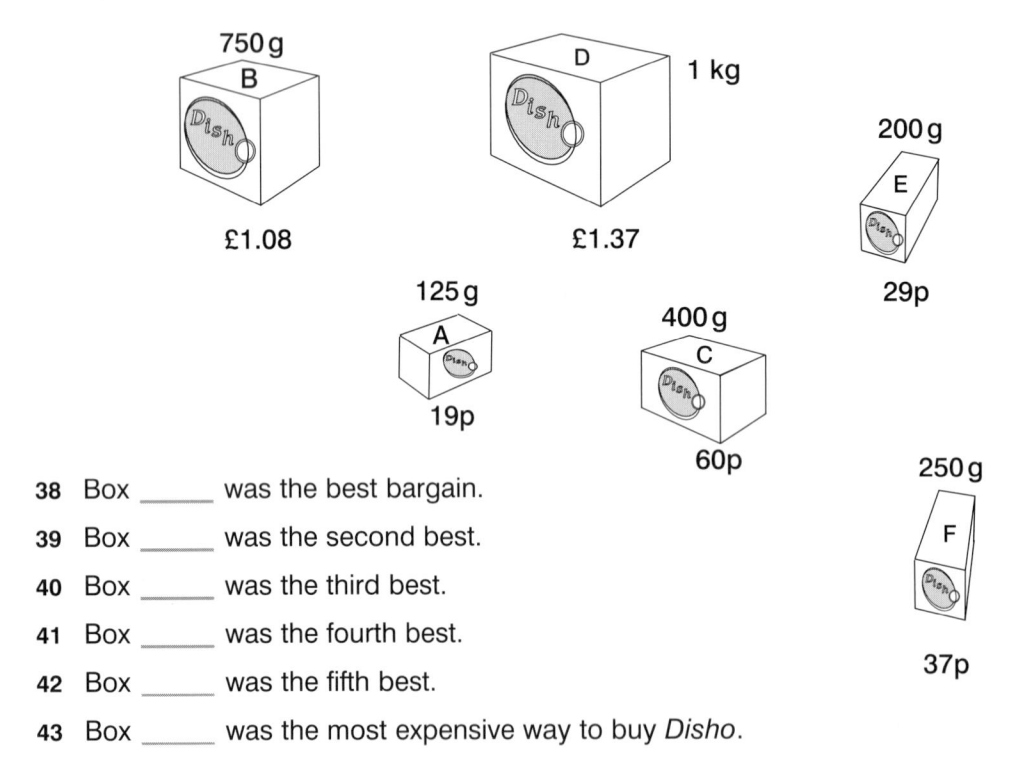

- B: 750 g — £1.08
- D: 1 kg — £1.37
- E: 200 g — 29p
- A: 125 g — 19p
- C: 400 g — 60p
- F: 250 g — 37p

38 Box _____ was the best bargain.
39 Box _____ was the second best.
40 Box _____ was the third best.
41 Box _____ was the fourth best.
42 Box _____ was the fifth best.
43 Box _____ was the most expensive way to buy *Disho*.

44 A coil of rope was divided into 7 equal sections, each 17.5 metres long.

If there were 3.25 m left, how long was the rope? _____

45 How many days were there between the 4th January and the 2nd March 2001?

Do not include either of the given dates. _____

46 A greenhouse can be bought by paying a deposit of £45, and then 12 monthly payments of £37.50.

What would be the total cost of the greenhouse? _____

47 How many fifths are there in $12\frac{4}{5}$?

48 What is the smallest number into which 6, 8, 10 and 12 will all divide without remainder?

49 The houses on Union Street are all on one side, and are numbered 1, 2, 3, 4 and so on.

If the house with the middle number is number 37, how many houses are there in the street?

50 Scarcroft United has 5000 spectators to watch their game this week.

Each stand seats 870.

What is the fewest number of stands required for this crowd?

Paper 23

1–10 Complete this multiplication table.

×				
	—	—	56	—
	—	—	35	—
	77			21
	11	9	—	—

Write the numbers below correct to the nearest 100.

11 71 246 _____

12 1486 _____

13 1274 _____

14 704.85 _____

15 What number is halfway between 98 and 144?

16–18 At Black Horse Junior School there were altogether 394 teachers and children.

The teachers and the boys numbered 189, and the girls and teachers together numbered 217.

There were _____ teachers, _____ boys and _____ girls.

19 Make 478 three hundred times as large.

♣ = a + 3

20–23 Complete this table.

a	__	1	__	3
♣	3	__	5	__

Look in the circle and find the answers to these questions.

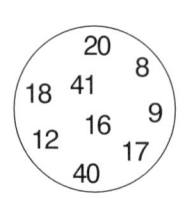

(circle contains: 20, 8, 18, 41, 16, 9, 12, 17, 40)

24 $9^2 - 8^2 =$ _____

25 $11^2 - 9^2 =$ _____

26 $2^3 + 2^2 =$ _____

27 $5^2 - 4^2 =$ _____

Find the area of these triangles.

The area of a triangle = $\frac{1}{2}$ (base × height)   1 square = 1 cm²

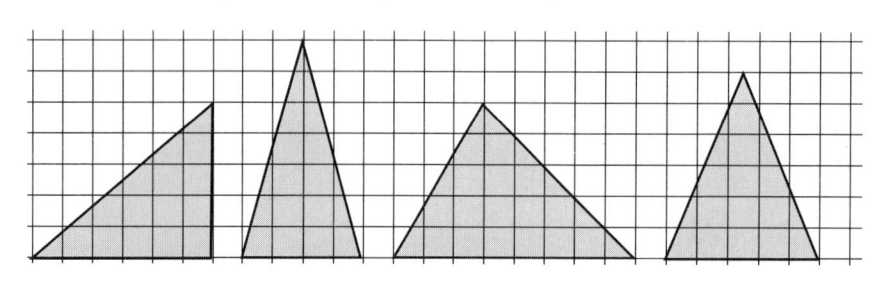

28 _____ **29** _____ **30** _____ **31** _____

Divide the year 2001 into 2 parts so that the second part is 4 times as large as the first part.

32 How many days are there in the shorter part? _____

33 In the larger part there are _____ days.

34 If the shorter section starts on January 1st, when does it end? _____

35 If $\frac{5}{12}$ of the contents of a box weigh 20 kg, what is the weight of all the contents? _____

36 What would $\frac{1}{8}$ of the contents weigh? _____

37–40 Fill in the missing numbers.

a	2	35	__	47	__
3a	6	__	231	__	267

Paper 4

1. 2 cm
2. 12 cm
3. 26 cm
4. 6 cm
5. 24 cm
6. 47
7. 0.01
8. 4
9. 0.01
10. 0.69
11. 1.21
12. 5.67
13. 36
14. 4365
15. 2**781**
16. **3**457
17. 1**071**
18. **2**85
19. 7
20. 342
21. 3
22. 4
23. 2
24. 3
25. $\frac{1}{2}$
26. $\frac{1}{2}$
27. $\frac{1}{6}$
28. $\frac{1}{6}$
29. $\frac{1}{3}$
30. $\frac{3}{7}$
31. $\frac{4}{7}$
32. 0
33. 37.7
34. 465
35. 1.26
36. 0.27
37. 490
38. 5670
39. 0.023
40. 7
41. 7
42. 20
43. 3.5
44. 19
45. 46
46. 5:05 a.m.
47. 12:45 p.m.
48. 8:02 p.m.
49. 3:15 p.m.
50. 11:14 a.m.

Paper 5

1–7

	Length	Width	Area
Rectangle 1	8 m	6 m	**48 m²**
Rectangle 2	**8 m**	4 m	32 m²
Rectangle 3	4 m	**2.5 m**	10 m²
Rectangle 4	**3 m**	3.5 m	10.5 m²
Rectangle 5	1.5 m	1.5 m	**2.25 m²**
Rectangle 6	5 m	**1.2 m**	6 m²
Rectangle 7	1.3 m	2 m	**2.6 m²**

8. 15 cm²
9. 30 cm²
10. 16 cm²
11. 10 cm²
12. 7:58 p.m.
13. Mathematics
14. English
15. 30
16. 7.5 or $7\frac{1}{2}$
17. 4
18. 8
19. 12
20. 16
21. 20
22. 24
23. £45
24. £99
25. £225
26. £36
27. £27
28. £252
29. 288
30. 72
31. 4
32. 14.6
33. 11 900
34. 1420
35. 213 000
36. 29.2
37. 47 600
38. 137
39. 9:13 p.m.
40. 0.3 km or 300 m
41. 0.1 km or 100 m
42. 0.03 km² or 30000 m²
43. 12 days
44. 1221
45. 74
46. 13
47. 17
48. 2
49. 3
50. 5

Paper 6

1. 37
2. 121
3. 95
4. 120°
5. 90°
6. 72°
7. 60°
8. 45°
9. 2.45
10. 13.42
11. 123.45
12. 1.357
13. 12.986
14. 0.456
15. 18
16. 12
17. 17
18. 1993

19–34

3	×	3	−	2	=	7
×	■	+	■	×	■	−
6	+	4	−	5	=	5
÷	■	−	■	−	■	×
2	×	5	−	4	=	6
=	■	=	■	=	■	=
9	×	2	−	6	=	12

35. £7.70
36. 7000
37. 6000
38. 7000
39. 5000
40. 6000
41. 5000
42. =
43. <
44. >
45. >
46. =
47. >
48. $\frac{2}{6}$ or $\frac{1}{3}$
49. 0
50. 1 or $\frac{6}{6}$

10–11 years

Paper 1

1. 15 min
2. 30 min
3. 30 min
4. 15 min
5. 30 min
6. 6
7. 4
8. 4
9. 9990
10. $\frac{1}{2}$ (smallest)
11. $\frac{7}{8}$ (largest)
12. 0.307 (smallest)
13. 37 (largest)
14. $\frac{10}{10}$ (smallest)
15. $\frac{15}{3}$ (largest)
16. 0.125 (smallest)
17. $\frac{7}{8}$ (largest)
18. $\frac{2}{5}$ of 10 (smallest)
19. $\frac{5}{7}$ of 14 (largest)
20. 10 2021
21. 169
22. 209
23. 389
24. 449
25. 60°
26. 150°
27. 120°
28. 30°
29. 180°
30. 5
31. 2
32. 3
33. 5
34–37

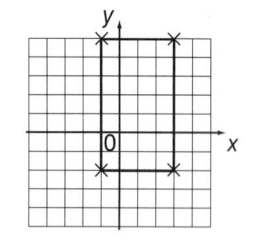

38. (−1,−2)
39. 21:45
40. 10:50
41. 12:55
42. 4
43. 12
44. 20
45. +
46. ÷
47. ×
48. ÷
49. 24
50. 28

Paper 2

1. 7.865
2. 0.654
3. 46.75
4. 0.0123
5. 49
6. 47
7. 45
8. 43
9. 185
10. 222
11. 40
12. 80
13. 60 miles
14. 50 miles
15. ÷
16. +
17. −
18. ×
19. $\frac{1}{2}$ or $\frac{3}{6}$
20. $\frac{1}{6}$
21. $\frac{1}{2}$ or $\frac{3}{6}$
22. 3
23. 5
24. 7
25. 30
26. 36
27. 9 cm^2
28. 9:00 p.m. or 21:00
29. 2:00 p.m. or 14:00
30. 1:00 p.m. or 13:00
31. 8:00 p.m. or 20:00
32. 03:00
33. 11:00
34. 11:00
35. 08:36
36. $\frac{17}{16}$ or $1\frac{1}{16}$
37. $2\frac{7}{9}$ or $\frac{25}{9}$
38. 20
39. 18
40. 3
41. 20
42. 3
43. 6
44. 4.5
45. 7.1
46. 3.09
47. 2661
48. 3402
49. 234
50. 15 960

Paper 3

1. 4
2. 25
3. 9
4. 36
5. 11:10
6. 11:45
7. 11:45
8. 12:20
9. 12:20
10. 12:55
11. 12:55
12. 1:10
13. 1:45
14. 1:45
15. 2:20
16. 988
17. 60 cm^2
18. 30 cm^2
19. 50 cm^2
20. 32 cm
21. 22 cm
22. 30 cm
23. 10
24. 5
25. 4
26. 5
27. £22
28. £18
29. £5.36
30. 6 cm^2
31. 12 cm^2
32. 10 cm^2
33. 12 cm^2
34. £3.50
35. £3.50
36. £5.25
37. £7.00
38. £35.00
39. £235.00
40. £70.00
41. £470.00
42. £52.50
43. £352.50
44. 8 m 11 cm
45. 2 m 94 cm
46. 23 m
47. 300
48. 800
49. 500
50. 1100

Paper 22

1. 22 m
2. 5.5 m
3. Ben
4. Ahmed
5. 7
6. Ben
7. 3
8. Ahmed
9. 14
10. 13
11. 14
12. 12
13. 0.7
14. 7
15. 70
16. 4230
17. 4230
18. 5230
19. 77
20. 75
21. 53
22. 49
23. 45
24. 51
25. 64
26. 49

27–32

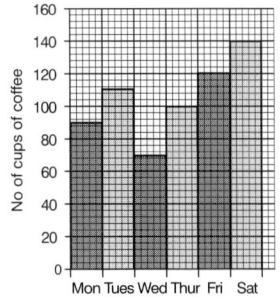

33. 10:23
34. 10:37
35. 10:50
36. 11:04
37. 11:29
38. D
39. B
40. E
41. F
42. C
43. A
44. 125.75 m
45. 56 days
46. £495
47. 64
48. 120
49. 73
50. 6

Paper 23

1–10

×	(11)	(9)	(7)	(3)
(8)	**88**	**72**	56	**24**
(5)	**55**	**45**	35	**15**
(7)	77	**63**	**49**	21
(1)	11	9	**7**	**3**

11. 71 200
12. 1500
13. 1300
14. 700
15. 121
16. 12
17. 177
18. 205
19. 143 400

20–23

a	**0**	**1**	**2**	**3**
♣	3	**4**	5	**6**

24. 17
25. 40
26. 12
27. 9
28. 15 cm²
29. 14 cm²
30. 20 cm²
31. 15 cm²
32. 73
33. 292
34. 14th March
35. 48 kg
36. 6 kg

37–40

a	2	35	**77**	47	**89**
3a	6	**105**	231	**141**	267

41. 311
42. 162
43. 18
44. £4.70
45. £16.45
46. 171
47. 3.125
48. 4.05
49. 7.625
50. 9.075

Paper 24

1. $\frac{7}{12}$
2. 8.01
3. 0.016
4. 200
5. 1.789
6. 540
7. 49 cm²
8. 7203

9–15

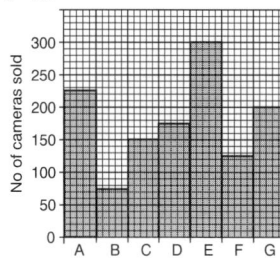

16. 80
17. £60
18. 33
19. 63
20. 1
21. 3
22. 7
23. 21
24. 3
25. 7
26. 29
27. £17
28. 10
29. 1000 or 10 000
30. 256 cm²
31. 112 cm²
32. 144 cm²
33. 64 cm
34. 64 cm
35. 0.3
36. 30%
37. 0.07
38. 7%
39. $\frac{1}{4}$
40. 25%
41. 0.05
42. 5%
43. 6.873
44. 19.05
45. £4.75
46. £58.85
47. £6.10
48. £38.75
49. £11.31
50. £1.12

A8

Paper 19

1. $7\frac{4}{5}$
2. $47\frac{1}{2}$
3. $31\frac{1}{4}$
4. $\frac{1}{8}$
5. 2650 m

6–13

×	(5)	(7)	(2)	(3)
(3)	**15**	**21**	6	9
(8)	**40**	56	16	24
(4)	20	**28**	8	12
(9)	45	63	**18**	**27**

14. 1.7
15. 1.43
16. 47
17. 0.007
18. 2590
19. 0.14
20. ×
21. ×
22. +
23. −
24. −
25. ÷
26. 100
27. 1.23
28. 13.6
29. 5
30. £52.50
31. £352.50
32. £26.25
33. £176.25
34. £10.50
35. £70.50
36. 3
37. 22
38. 6
39. 20
40. 2
41. 28
42. 50%
43. 16%
44. no
45. yes
46. no
47. no
48. no
49. no
50. yes

Paper 20

1. Laser
2. Spaceship
3. Galaxy
4. Spaceship
5. £8.60
6. £2.15
7. 29%
8. 5121
9. 4021
10. 8080
11. 433

12–14

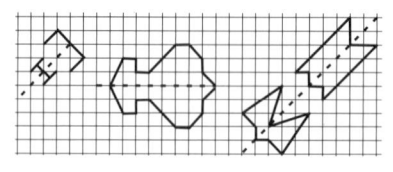

15. 6
16. 1
17. 4
18. 2
19. 5
20. 3
21. 51
22. £5.10
23. 821.5 g
24. 143
25. 225
26. 8^2
27. 234
28. 168

29–41

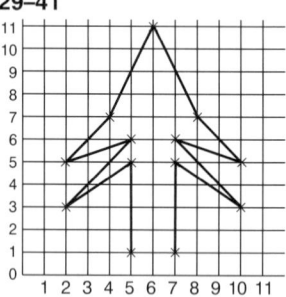

42. a tree

43–48

Ocean	square km	square miles
Atlantic	82 200 000	31 700 000
Indian	73 480 000	28 360 000
Pacific	165 000 000	64 000 000

49. 70
50. 490

Paper 21

1. even
2. odd
3. even
4. even
5. £2
6. £3
7. £5
8. £6
9. £8
10. 45p
11. 1 hr 10 min
12. 1 hr 35 min
13. 2 hr
14. 2 hr 25 min
15. 2 hr 50 min
16. 3 hr 15 min
17. 0.374
18. 0.0148
19. 0.00255
20. 189
21. 231
22. £4.80
23. £3
24. £1.20
25. $\frac{5}{6}$
26. $\frac{3}{4}$
27. $\frac{7}{12}$
28. $\frac{11}{24}$
29. $\frac{3}{8}$
30. mile
31. pint
32. ounce
33. feet
34. 8:20 p.m.
35. 8:05 a.m.
36. 12:10 a.m.
37. 5:45 p.m.
38. 53
39. 9
40. 10
41. 9
42. £1.05
43. 14
44. 42
45. 84
46. 12
47. 33
48. 3
49. 9
50. 6

41 By how much is the product of 27 and 13 greater than their sum?

There are 180 sheep in a flock.
For every 9 white sheep there is 1 black sheep.

42 How many white sheep are there?

43 How many black sheep are there?

Mr Pin paid £7.05 for 1.5 metres of material.

44 What was the cost per metre?

45 How much would 3.5 m cost?

46 What is the next odd number after 160 into which 9 will divide without remainder?

47–50 Write these fractions in decimal form.

$3\frac{1}{8}$ $\quad$ $4\frac{1}{20}$ $\quad$ $7\frac{5}{8}$ $\quad$ $9\frac{3}{40}$

Paper 24

Underline the correct answer in each line.

1 $\frac{1}{3} + \frac{1}{4}$	=	$\frac{1}{7}$	$\frac{7}{12}$	$\frac{2}{7}$	$\frac{2}{12}$
2 $10 - 1.99$	=	9.11	8.01	11.99	9.01
3 0.04×0.4	=	0.016	0.16	0.08	0.0016
4 $4 \div 0.02$	=	20	2	0.2	200
5 $17.89 \div 10$	=	178.9	1789	1.789	17.89
6 2.7×200	=	5.4	540	54.0	0.54

7 The perimeter of a square is 28 cm. What is its area?

8
$\quad\quad\quad\quad$ 147
$\quad\quad\times\;\;$ 49
$\quad\quad\quad\quad$ ———

$\quad\quad\quad\quad$ ———

9–15 On the squared paper draw a bar chart to show the following information.

Shop	A	B	C	D	E	F	G
Cameras sold	225	75	150	175	300	125	200

Be careful to use a scale which will show this information accurately.

Write in your scale.

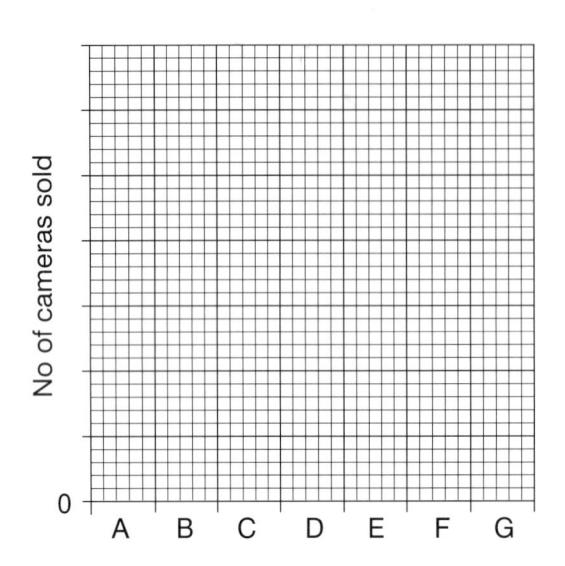

16 How many tiles, each 50 cm × 50 cm, would be needed to cover a floor 5 metres × 4 metres? _____

17 What would be the cost of these tiles if I had to pay £7.50 for 10 tiles? _____

18–19 Put a circle around the non-prime numbers.

    3   13   23   33   43   53   63

20–23 What are the factors of 21? ____ , ____ , ____ , ____

24–25 Underline the prime factors of 21.

    2   3   4   5   6   7   8

26 How many times can 34 be subtracted from 986? _____

Ted has £98 and Tom has £64.

27 How much must Ted give to Tom so that will each have the same amount? _____

28 Would you estimate the number of children in a class to the nearest 10, 100, 1000? _____

29 Would you estimate the number of people at a Premier League football game to the nearest 10, 1000, 10 000 or 1 000 000? _____

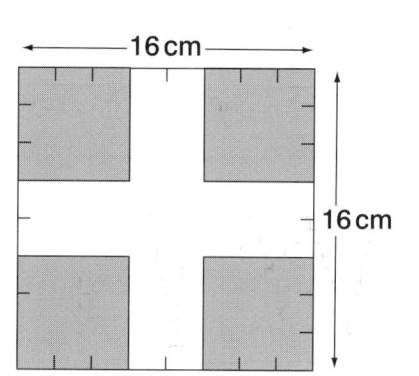

30 The area of the flag is _____ .

31 The area of the cross is _____ .

32 The shaded part has an area of _____ .

33 The perimeter of the flag is _____ .

34 The perimeter of the cross is _____ .

35–42 Complete the following table.

Fraction	Decimal	Percentage
3/10	_____	_____
7/100	_____	_____
_____	0.25	_____
1/20	_____	_____

43 $8 - 1.127 =$ _____

44 $47.625 \div 2.5 =$ _____

45–50 Complete the following table.

Wholesale price	Retail price	Profit
£18.75	£23.50	_____
_____	£70.20	£11.35
£5.13	_____	97p
£196.50	£235.25	_____
_____	£13.50	£2.19
93p	_____	19p

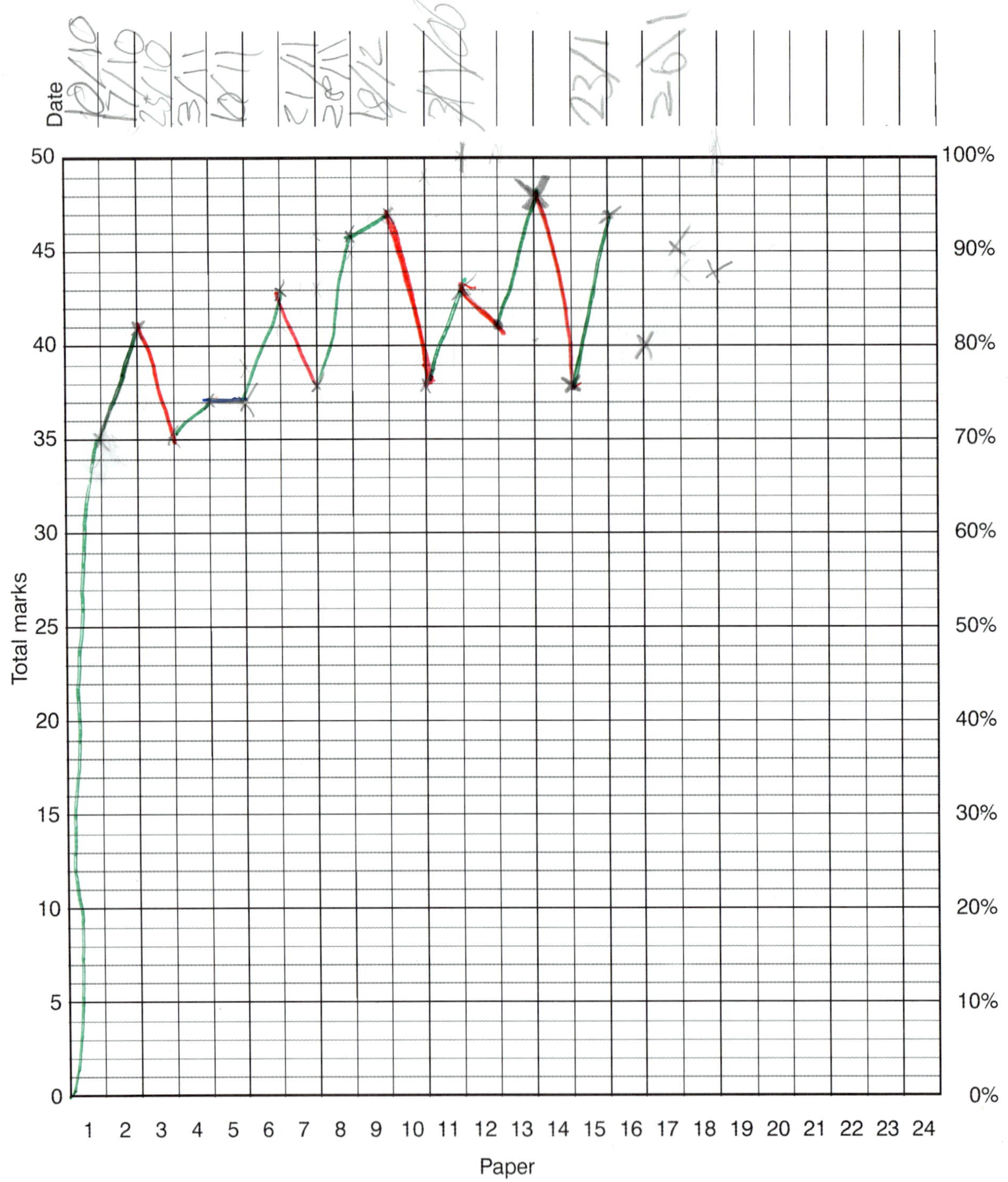
Date
Total marks
0
5
10
15
20
25
30
35
40
45
50
0%
10%
20%
30%
40%
50%
60%
70%
80%
90%
100%
1 2 3 4 5 6 7 8 9 10 11 12 13 14 15 16 17 18 19 20 21 22 23 24
Paper